The **Vital** *Few*
versus
The **Trivial** *Many*

Invest with the Insiders, Not the Masses

George Muzea

WILEY

John Wiley & Sons, Inc.

For general information on our other products and services, or technical support,
please contact our Customer Care Department within the United States at 800-762-
2974, outside the United States at 317-572-3993 or fax 317-572-4002.

Wiley also publishes its books in a variety of electronic formats. Some content that
appears in print may not be available in electronic books.

For more information about Wiley products, visit our web site at www.wiley.com.

ISBN: 0-471-68195-4

Printed in the United States of America.

10 9 8 7 6 5 4 3 2 1

*To my father, Pandely Muzea, a self-made man
who inspired me to be the best I could become*

*To my mother, Angelina Muzea, still going strong
at 102, who taught me to put others' interests before mine*

*To my wife, Maria, who provided me with the love
and support I needed to write this book*

Contents

Contents

Contents

Preface

What is life?
It is the flash of a firefly in the night.
It is the breath of a buffalo in the wintertime.
It is the little shadow that runs across the grass
and loses itself in the sunset.
—Crowfoot

I LOVE THE ABOVE QUOTE BY THE GREAT INDIAN CHIEF CROWFOOT. IT is a constant reminder to me to not waste my or anyone else's time. Time is a precious commodity and one that we all run out of far too soon. Crowfoot's quote made me realize as I reached Social Security age that if I was ever going to give back some of the knowledge I had learned in life and in business, especially in the stock market, I had better start now.

My book is a unique look at contrarian investing, designed to help the individual investor make money in the stock market, and most importantly, not to give back his or her hard-earned gains at market tops.

In the following pages, I discuss different investing styles, solutions to mistakes that many investors make in managing their money, how to follow The Vital Few (corporate insiders), and how to avoid getting mislead by so-called experts who incorrectly influence the masses or The Trivial Many.

Acknowledgments

I'D LIKE TO THANK THOSE WHOSE CONTRIBUTIONS MADE THIS BOOK possible:

Joyce Griffith, for her wonderful ideas and editing of my autobiography. Although I didn't include it in this book, I did use many of the personal anecdotes to illustrate how my contrarian philosophy evolved.

All of the magnificent editors at John Wiley & Sons, especially Executive Editor Debra Englander, who supported and guided me throughout the project.

My many Magic T subscribers who have so loyally supported my work and given me ideas for this revised and updated version of *The Vital Few versus The Trivial Many* (originally a small self-published book).

My wife, Maria, for her capable editing and many excellent suggestions about the content. I also want to thank her for giving me a chance to show her that I was worthy enough for her to share her life with me. It hasn't always been easy. I was 56 years old when we married (my first marriage). One week after we were married, we found out that I had a son living in Holland that I didn't know about. Marcus had a wife and two daughters. That was 10 years ago. Since then we all have become extremely close, and throughout, Maria has been a bastion of love and support. I love and worship her.

Introduction

I STARTED MY CAREER IN THE INVESTMENT BUSINESS IN 1966. Over the years, it became clear to me that many investors, individual and professional, consistently lost money in the stock market. For the first 10 years of my career, I was also in the loser's camp, selling out at the bottom and buying in at the top. I always seemed to do the wrong thing, especially at market turning points.

After discovering there were investors who always seemed to be stock market winners, I decided I would devote my life to finding ways to ferret out these smarter investors. I named them The Vital Few. In order to compare what The Vital Few were doing at key stock market turning points to the actions of the consistent losers, like myself, I needed to find ways to monitor the losing investors. I named this group The Trivial Many.

Soon after I had learned how to monitor both The Vital Few and The Trivial Many, I became a consistent stock market winner. It really was not that difficult. The hardest part was admitting to myself that I was, in fact, a stock market loser. After I had accepted that fact, I was determined to find out why and how to correct the problem.

I am confident that my book will give you a new way of looking at the investing world, especially the stock market. Since uncovering the secrets I outline here, it has been a lucrative and interesting journey for me. I am confident it will be for you as well.

CHAPTER 1

Key Reasons
Investors Lose Money

THE STOCK MARKET DECLINE IN 2001 AND 2002 CONVINCED MANY investors that the market is an impossible place to make money consistently over time. Nothing could be further from the truth; actually, it has never been easier. Before I tell you my secret to becoming a consistent winner in the stock market, we need to examine some of the key reasons investors lose money.

The first mistake: investing without a plan or using the wrong investment strategy. Many investors have no plan for making money in the stock market. Others use the wrong strategies because they fail to see changes in market trends. Sports teams, corporations, and organizations that achieve success always work from a fundamentally sound plan. It is no different for those who want to succeed in the stock market.

In golf, the most important part of the game is to develop a pre-shot routine that includes good balance and setup. At the golf club where I play, I frequently see PGA golfers in the exercise room working on their setup and balance. It is amazing to me just how still they can be on a small balance beam. Investors, like golfers, need a consistent routine as well. In the financial world, this is known as an investment style.

There are three basic styles of investing: value, growth, and momentum, and there are many variations within these styles.

The most common investment style is value investing. Value investing offers the lowest risk of any other style of investing. Value investors are known as bargain hunters, looking for stocks priced low in comparison to the company's historical earnings and growth prospects. The most common strategy for a value investor is to buy a stock when it is undervalued relative to its earnings history and prospects and then sell it when it is fully valued. With a long-term approach, the value investor will see many stocks go through cycles of overvaluation and undervaluation.

Undervaluation has been the key to success for Warren Buffett and his company, Berkshire Hathaway, whose shares began selling in 1967 at $12/share. The world's most famous value investor once said, "The most common cause of low prices is pessimism . . . sometimes specific to a company or industry. We want to do business in such an environment, not because we like pessimism but because we like the prices it produces. It's optimism that is the enemy of the rational buyer."

Unlike Warren Buffett, who is a bottom-up stock analyst, I have always been more of a top-down strategist. This puts me at a disadvantage when it comes to buying depressed, undervalued stocks. I am simply not as well trained in security analysis to ferret out undervalued stocks as Buffett and his analysts are.

Analytically and financially, I am no match for Buffett. However, I have found that my knowledge of insider trading helps me make up for my lack of traditional analytical skills. When I see a stock on the new low list or one that is being panned in the media, I always look to see what insiders are doing. In the 1980s, I was perusing a friend's copy of *Value Line*. I noticed that Global Marine was listed as a 5, a strong sell signal. The *Value Line* analysis indicated that the stock had a terrible balance sheet and had negative cash flow. I was not sure at the time what that meant, but it sounded bad. In those days, I had no historical insider data on stocks and there was no Internet to check insider trading. I did, however, have access to insider trading reported to the New York Stock Exchange. I discovered that six insiders had bought approximately 275,000 shares in the $3 area. I reasoned that if these insiders were buying a stock with such bad fundamentals, maybe there was something going on that was unrecognized by traditional Wall Street research. Three years later, I sold the stock at $27, just about the time that *Value Line* had raised its rating to 1, its strongest signal, citing the company's improved fundamentals. *Value Line* was right, and the stock moved up another 30 percent. I have never been a great seller, but I like making the easy money by getting in early.

Income investing is a form of value investing that deserves mention. Also known as dividend investing, this is a straightforward strategy designed to pick stocks that provide a steady stream of income. There are two types of investors seeking income—equity income investors who buy stocks that pay dividends and fixed income investors who buy corporate and municipal bonds and other fixed income alternatives.

Typically, income investors focus on the dividend yield of well-established companies with very predictable earnings streams. The risk of buying historically high dividend paying stocks and holding them for the long term is very low. Dividend distribution and the levels of payouts, however, depend on the retained earnings of the company. It is always wise to make sure there is a large spread between a company's latest 12-month earnings and the amount of the dividend. Cushions are great to rest your head on, and a good cushion between the amount of earnings a company makes and its projected dividends can help you sleep comfortably.

Growth investing is the practice of buying fast-growing companies with high potential. The basic strategy for a growth investor is to buy a company with gains in earnings per share of 15 to 20 percent annually. Many growth investors are drawn to the high-tech industries such as telecommunications and the Internet with aggressive management, such as Intel and Microsoft, and innovative leading technology companies. Young companies with top-notch management, often creating superior brands like Internet leaders AOL and Amazon.com also attract growth investors.

Most growth stocks, however, are very risky because of the public's willingness to pay premium prices, which inflates the P/E ratios. Vulnerability to changes in perception of the growth potential or to a downtrend of investor confidence in that growth can cause the P/E ratios of these stocks to drop dramatically. The company's industry may play a part in the risk level as well due to varying growth averages and valuations. Stock selection is the most important factor in the strategy for growth investors, using screening programs filtering projected earnings growth against historical earnings.

Growth at a Reasonable Price (GARP) investing combines the two successful strategies of value and growth investing into a very sensible stock picking approach. GARP investors buy only stocks with growth at a reasonable price, operating in a more traditional mode than value investors, who look for stocks that are relatively cheap in relation to the company's earnings and book value, and growth investors, who buy stocks that tend to grow substantially fast and have high earnings potential.

After the dot-com crash, GARP became the popular acronym on Wall Street. The aftermath of the Internet sell-off presented some good buying opportunities, but the bottom for companies like Cisco and Yahoo!, classic growth stocks, hit further down the road. Traditionally, GARP investors seek growth companies with solid growth prospects and share prices that are somewhat lower than their intrinsic value, stopping short of looking at the company's business in detail. However, by November 2000, Cisco had lost more than 50 percent of its value, and Yahoo! had dropped from $120 to $15. Even though there was nothing fundamentally wrong with these companies, market conditions at that time could not help a GARP investor. The Magic T discussed in Chapter 13 is designed to identify market tops and bottoms, which can help GARP and other investors with market timing.

The world's most famous growth investor, Peter Lynch, defined growth at a reasonable price without ever even calling it GARP in his strategic practice to pay no more than one times the growth rate of earnings per share over the past three to five years as well as the projected earnings over the next three to five years. Similar to value investing, the analysis of insider trading of individual growth stocks can help investors discover which stocks to buy. When insiders purchase the shares of growth stocks at higher and higher prices, good news usually follows. Good or better than expected news is the fuel that keeps growth stocks growing. Insider trading will be discussed in greater detail in Chapter 5.

The third broad investing style and probably the most popular with younger investors is momentum investing. The fundamental tenet of momentum investing is that investments, whether they are stocks or industries that have already outperformed the market in the past, are likely to continue their winning ways. This belief builds on the notion that most investors are like cattle and will tend to herd with the most recent winners. Momentum investors chase the hot stocks and funds, and they do not mind swinging from the fences. For them, 15 percent or 20 percent returns in a year is not worth talking about. They want doubles and triples within a few months.

Most momentum investors will tell you that they focus on companies with accelerating earnings, better than expected earnings, analyst upgrades, and stocks that are increasing faster than the market. Many momentum investors have strong disciplines, and I know some money managers who use this strategy very profitably. It is fine, in my opinion, to let them manage your money if you are so inclined—just not in a bear market.

It is the bear market that clobbers momentum investors and puts them into hibernation. In 2000, for example, investors discovered that markets can and do become simultaneous and illiquid, which killed the notion that momentum players can get out at any time. When bad news hits a momentum stock or industry, the door shuts just as everyone is trying to escape.

In early 2004, I was increasingly concerned with the lack of insider buying and the fact that just about everyone I spoke to was charting stocks and talking about momentum. I recall one of my firm's young money managers telling me that his approach was simple. As a proponent of William O'Neil, who many consider the father of the momentum style, he bought every stock that broke out of a base on high volume and added to his position when it pulled back to support levels on light volume. I muttered to myself that it seemed like déjà vu all over again. Hadn't anyone learned from the bursting of the bubble in 2000?

The problem with momentum investing is that it works best during the early to middle stages of a stock increase or overall market advances. At some point in time, there will be a final breakout to new highs that most likely will be the top for the cycle and could be the top for many years. How does a momentum investor know whether the last breakout to new high ground is not the top?

One thing I know for sure, though: You can always count on the return of momentum investors. Most have short memories and the next bull market will bring them back in force again. Greed is human nature and, in my opinion, momentum investing personifies greed.

No discussion of momentum investing would be complete without discussing CANSLIM. This is a philosophy developed by William O'Neil, co-founder of *Investors Business Daily*, focusing on earnings and overall strength of momentum companies. The acronym spells out the criterion for this stock selection process.

- Current quarterly earnings must be up at least 18 percent.
- Annual earnings per share should show growth over the past five years.
- New highs in price are achieved as a result of new significant industry conditions.
- Shares outstanding should be at a small and reasonable number.
- Leading the industry or, better yet, the market.
- Institutional sponsorship from firms with above average recent performance.
- Market indexes and the market's overall current direction have been determined.

These are the fundamental characteristics of historically successful stocks. The CANSLIM strategy is strict; all the above criteria must be met to warrant an investment. It includes practices from all the major investment strategies but does not support investing into high-risk companies.

My investment style is simple; it is a top-down strategy. I want to be in the stock market when the odds are in my favor and out when the odds are against me. For picking stocks, I buy both growth and value stocks, but only if there is insider buying to support the picture. I want to be a partner—not an adversary—with the men and women whose companies I invest in.

As we examine some of the key reasons investors lose money, here is the second mistake: following investment market letter writers and so-called experts who appear in the media, especially in television. Most market letter writers and other experts are wrong more than they are right, especially at key market turning points. Following them is a prescription for disaster.

The third mistake: investing at the wrong time. Believe it or not, starting an investment plan in certain months will almost always guarantee failure. The good news is that in other months, investors are almost guaranteed success, given the right plan.

Clearly, if you can correct these mistakes, you will be well on your way to being a consistent stock market winner.

CHAPTER 2

Solution to Mistake #1: Use the Right Strategy

THE FIRST THING YOU MUST DO TO BE A WINNER IN THE STOCK market is to develop a sound investing strategy, one that you can stick with because, among other things, you believe in its principles.

Since 60 percent of all stock price movements are related to the trend of the overall market, the right strategy must be one that begins at the top and works down. You must know what the risk/reward is at all times for successful investing. To do this, you must be brutally honest with yourself.

I visit many money managers around the country, and I am amazed by how much paper they have on their desks. How in the world can they process all this input? The reality is that most cannot. The human mind can handle only so much data at one time. Nobel laureate Herbert Simon said, "Millions of new bits of information hit our environment every second."

There are two types of reasoning processes we use to function in life. One is linear, in which our thoughts travel from one point to another in a logical sequence similar to building a home from a set of blueprints within a given timeline. The other type of reasoning is interactive. This is more complex, whereby each separate piece of information used in reaching a decision affects the other pieces and may not even be available at the same time. For example, if we plan to start a business, we have to know if there is a demand for our product and what the costs will be to make it, taking into account the availability of qualified workers, the anticipated revenues, and the current and future trends of the economy. All of these variables, and more, must be considered if we are to be successful.

Many people are very good at interactive reasoning. If you are one of those people who can multitask, you would be good at interactive reasoning. However, while these talents would be useful in many business situations, they are useless in the stock market. Each piece of information required to make money in the market interacts with all the other pieces. Some of these elements include: the current Federal Reserve policy and its impact on interest rates, political events, foreign affairs, war, oil shortages, terrorism, and the trend of the economy where you live. All of these events affect the stock market in some way. The problem is that most of them are out of your control.

Further proof that interactive reasoning is ill suited for the type of analysis required to be successful in the stock market is the record of market experts. In the past 51 years, more than 50 surveys have been made by experts forecasting their favorite stocks and industries. Expert selections underperformed the stock market 75 percent of the time!

Use the Right Strategy

When I managed a large stock brokerage office in Boston, I used to tell the brokers that they could not control the market. The only thing they could control was their work habits. The reality is that the human mind, or even a computer for that matter, cannot process all the information that is coming from the market, and how each piece relates to other pieces. Our minds, in effect, lead us to failure in the stock market.

Since the stock market requires a certain type of reasoning that is impossible for our minds to utilize, you could say we were born to lose in the stock market. There is a solution, however. Knowing that we have no chance, we have to ask ourselves if the market letter writers and the financial media know they are destined to be wrong as well. They do not; it is only their job to advise and appear as experts.

Our brains must use interactive reasoning to process all the information that affects stock prices and market trends. We cannot do it all and we know it. On the other hand, market experts such as those seen on television and the hundreds of market letter writers who influence public opinion do not know they are doomed to failure.

So the first part of our strategy is to not follow experts. Then, once we have determined what the majority of these experts are saying, we can safely do the opposite!

I began my investment career in 1966 as a stockbroker with E.F. Hutton. As a new broker, I was encouraged to use the firm's recommended list to pick stocks for my clients. It did not take long for me to become disillusioned. It seemed to me that at the bottom of every bear market, the entire recommended list was on the new low list! I knew I would become an ex-stockbroker soon unless I found a better way to make money other than to use the system offered by the firm's research analysts.

Beginning in 1972, I started plotting charts of the stocks in Hutton's recommended list. I focused my attention on those stocks the firm liked that were already in up-trends. This helped considerably for a few years. However, the bear market of 1973–1974 destroyed that theory. Charting stocks was useful in picking stocks, but it failed to help me with the big economic picture. The term for this in the investment community is "macro analysis," a top-down approach to investing. Macro analysis assumes that if you are correct on the trend of the economy, and the overall trend of the stock market, you can take positions when the time is most favorable and avoid the stock market at other times. This made a lot of sense to me, but I was clueless as to how to do it.

I told you earlier that 60 percent of an individual stock's price movement is related to the overall trend of the market. After all, the major macro players on Wall Street were also experts and I knew that macro analysis also used interactive reasoning, which did not work. Therefore, I could not trust the macro experts, either. It seemed there was nowhere to turn and I was doomed to investment mediocrity.

I have always felt providentially guided. It seemed whenever I needed an answer to a life problem, it turned up. This time it came to me in an article I read about the history of Vilfredo Pareto.

Vilfredo Federico Damaso Pareto was a nineteenth-century

Italian economist who observed that a large percent of the national wealth in Italy was held by a small number of people. Pareto found that 80 percent of the land in Rome was owned by 20 percent of the population. Even as a gardener, he observed that 80 percent of the peas were harvested from 20 percent of the peapods. In modern times, the same concept exists in business, and in many other places as well. Most business managers will tell you that 80 percent of the sales and profits are generated by 20 percent of the people in their company, while at the same time 80 percent of a company's problems are caused by 20 percent of their employees.

Pareto himself could not have predicted that this simple ratio would be applied and restated thousands of times in boardrooms and business offices around the world, with managers referring to it as the Pareto Principle, the 80:20 Rule, and The Vital Few and The Trivial Many Rule. I had never seen anyone apply Pareto's ratio to the stock market, but I reasoned that since it worked so well in business, it could be very valuable in analyzing the stock market.

My father used to tell me it is alright to be average or below average at something, but do not be unaware of it. Once I had inferred that success in the stock market required a certain type of reasoning that was impossible for the human mind to utilize, I had to admit I was a loser in the stock market, and it would logically follow that everyone who followed my advice would also be a loser. I also knew that there were experts out there who could not or would not admit they were losers, too. These experts and the millions of investors they influenced were The Trivial Many. It was this group that I would bet against in the future. At important turning points, I knew they had to be wrong; otherwise

Pareto's principles were invalid. Logic told me Vilfredo Pareto had made an important human nature observation, and my new investment strategy was beginning to take shape.

I had identified who The Trivial Many were. To complete my strategy, I only had to find out who were The Vital Few. That is when my guardian angel came to my rescue again. I was living in Fort Lauderdale, Florida, and had just left E.F. Hutton for Dean Witter. One of the brokers in the office invited me to a local stock and bond club meeting. The formal meeting was preceded by a cocktail hour. During the party, I noticed a small middle-aged man wearing a bow tie. He looked somewhat out of place, but he had sort of a wry smile on his face, as if he knew a valuable secret. Approaching him, I introduced myself, and he told me his name was Perry Wysong. We exchanged pleasantries and in a short time began talking about the stock market.

I was amazed to find that Perry ran a small private fund of $25 million. He told me he was averaging 25 percent a year. He did not look like the type of person who would play one-upmanship, so I asked him to explain his methodology. He told me he followed corporate insiders.

Instantly, a bell rang in my head. Who knew better what was going on in companies than the officers and directors? It made perfect sense. Perry went on to explain that many university studies show that insiders outperform the stock market by a wide margin, consistently over time. The minute he explained how he did it, I was hooked. I had found The Vital Few!

That was in 1977. Over the next five years, Perry and I would meet for lunch and talk primarily about insiders. He loved the concept, and I was rapidly becoming one of his disciples. I told him I wanted to develop my own strategy for following insiders. He told me he would be happy to help me become successful. Perry was my friend and idol until the day he died, and I have always been grateful for his generosity.

With Perry's help, I began using my new investment strategy. I would use stocks bought by insiders when market conditions were favorable. A favorable market condition was when letter writers and experts were negative and insiders were positive. For the first time in my life, my clients were consistently making money. Many told me they had never been out of the stock market prior to a broad decline. They relished buying against the grain of public opinion when stocks were deeply depressed.

From 1978 to 1986, I hosted my own television show in South Florida called *The Muzea Insider Report*. I became known in Fort Lauderdale as Mr. Insider. Not only was I making a lot of money for my clients, I was truly enjoying myself. I retired from the brokerage business in 1986 at the age of 47. By then I was able to live off my principal gains and continued to utilize my investment strategy on my own.

Let us stop for a moment here and review what I have told you so far.

- Everyone needs an investment strategy or style that is easy to follow and produces consistent profits.
- The only way to consistently make money in the stock market is to go against the grain of public opinion. The Pareto

21

Principle works. Going against the 80 percent (public) and with the 20 percent (insiders) is the answer.

- Since the key to this strategy is to invest in the stock market only when the Vital Few are buying and The Trivial Many are selling, it is obvious that you must be willing to stay out of the stock market for long periods of time. Only losers bet on every horse race. It is the same with stocks.

In subsequent chapters, I spell out my entire strategy on becoming a consistent winner in the stock market, but first we need to go over the second and third mistakes made by most investors.

CHAPTER 3

Solution to Mistake #2: Understand the Correct Way to Follow Market Letter Writers and Media Experts

MY DISTRUST OF EXPERTS OF ANY KIND DEVELOPED EARLY IN MY LIFE, and nothing that has happened to me over the years has altered my views. I witnessed one of the most poignant examples of the failure of experts to make the right decision when I was a young naval officer serving on the aircraft carrier USS *Wasp*.

In 1960, one of the modern wonders of the military world at that time was a series of offshore Distant Early Warning (DEW) radar towers belonging to the government, which encircled the country to protect us from surprise attack by enemy forces.

The sea-based towers were called Texas Towers because they resembled the oil rigs in the offshore oil fields of Texas. At a cost of $21 million, the fourth Texas Tower was a marvel of modern science, six stories high and equipped with a swimming pool, recreation hall, and full facilities to house 90 men. Under the command of the Air Force the three-sided tower was planted on the ocean floor beneath 180 feet of water 65 miles off the New Jersey coast. The tower underwent a crew reduction to 28 men in November 1960. It was nicknamed Old Shaky after high winds from Hurricane Donna battered the tower, apparently weakening its supports.

On January 15, 1961, the USS *Wasp* was returning to Boston Harbor after sea operations. A fierce storm was spewing waves onto our deck, but we had managed to avoid the worst of the high winds and were not terribly concerned—until we heard "May Day!" signals. Receiving an urgent message that the Texas Tower was in trouble, we headed toward it. I knew that at about 7 miles an hour, it would take a long time for our ship to cover even the short distance of 35 miles.

As we made our way, we caught another "May Day!" signal, and with that the image vanished from our radar. The last words we heard from the tower were, "Thank God the *Wasp* is on its way." With no warning, the Texas Tower snapped and toppled into the ocean, hurling 28 servicemen to their deaths. We had come within 7 miles of the tower by then. I learned later that it had begun tilting wildly back and forth in high winds long before the SOS. Our commanding officer felt it would stand until dawn and that an anticipated lull in the storm would give us an oppor-tunity to evacuate the structure safely.

I was living in my own world of terror. I had never seen the sea that angry. Our deck was being washed by 35-foot-high waves, and on the bridge of the ship where I was deployed, I had a bird's eye view of the power of an ocean whipped to a fury by a deadly storm. The top of the flight deck was about 60 feet above sea level, and from there it was another 50 feet to the bridge. When the bow of the ship went down, I could see the waves crashing onto the ship and splashing water everywhere.

Our planes were battened down in the ship's hangars where the angled deck had allowed us to stow them safely. Most of our men were below deck, but the ship was rocking in the storm, and it was a terrifying scene. The front of the deck was torn up and the metal exterior on the ship's hull was dented.

We were organized into 4 teams of officers, with each team taking a 4-hour watch every 12 hours. These watches were in addition to my regular duties as a 1st Division officer, and consequently I did not have much time to eat or sleep.

Early in the morning, a few hours after the Texas Tower disaster, I headed for the bunk bed room in Boys' Town. We heard that Commander Donald Spaulding was looking for an officer to volunteer his services on a rescue boat to search for bodies.

Nobody wanted to go. We did not feel secure in our bunk beds with the sea pitching the ship from side to side, much less riding in a round 22-foot lifeboat we called the Whale Boat. The commander would say, "Safe as a slow turn on a merry-go-round," but we did not see it that way. The horrifying events were still vivid in our minds, and the storm was still lashing out.

Some of the men scrambled to the top of the bunk beds where they could reach the dozen or so light bulbs in the ceiling and quickly loosened each one, plunging the windowless room into total darkness. I was 23 years old and scared. I knew that if the commander couldn't get an officer to volunteer, he would order one to duty, and with my luck, it just might be me. I headed for the safest place I knew—huddled next to the floor beneath my bed.

No sooner had I slid under the bunk than Commander

Spaulding opened the door to our room and reached for the light switch. Nothing happened. We were all breathing softly.

"I need one volunteer to search for bodies in the area near the tower!" he bellowed. "Who will go?"

A long pause was finally broken by the firm voice of an officer in the bunk bed across the aisle from me. It was George Meyers, a graduate of Kings Point Merchant Marine Academy. "I'll go, Sir."

At that moment I did not know the full extent of the tragedy of the Texas Tower, but I knew it was deadly out there and that I did not want to risk my life a few miles off shore in the Atlantic Ocean. A few hours later, Meyers and the crew of rescue workers made it back safely but had managed to recover only one body at the site of the wreckage.

Over the years, I have often wondered why the Air Force did not remove those 28 men from the tower after Hurricane Donna had weakened the supports. Apparently heavy braces were added on the advice of engineering experts, and they concluded that the tower was up to its original strength. That might have been true, but the new braces actually created greater mass for high winds to weaken the tower and cause it to topple over.

The demise of Texas Tower Number Four further increased my disdain for the opinions of experts and analysts, which fueled my desire to ferret out the actions of The Vital Few and compare them to The Trivial Many.

Forty years after the Texas Tower tragedy, in the summer of 2001, my wife Maria and I were visiting her parents in Florida, and I noticed a car with a USS *Wasp* sticker on it. Intrigued, I knocked on his door. A man in his seventies answered and I told him I had been a crew member on the *Wasp* from 1960 to 1963. Ten ships had been commissioned by the Navy under the name,

USS *Wasp*, and he had been on the seventh, serving in WWII. He told me there was a society of *Wasp* alumni, and he helped me get in touch with the group through the Internet.

Not long after signing up, I received an e-mail from Don Abbott, a man whose father had been on the Texas Tower that night and had lost his life. Abbott's comments brought a lump to my throat.

"The man your whale boat picked up at the tower site was Master Sergeant Tray F. Williams," he wrote. Abbott added, "When Williams lost his life, his wife Betty was left with four young children to care for. Our families tried to comfort each other in our time of loss. Betty Williams passed away earlier this year."

Abbott told me that a second man had actually been recovered a few days later, Master Sergeant Ronald Baake. He had been the medic on the tower and the officer who had sent out the SOS in the hope of being rescued. Baake had been in the Navy before becoming an Air Force airman and in between those services he had been a Marine. When the tower went down, most of the other men were trying to throw off safes with military secrets in them. Everyone was washed overboard except Sergeant Baake; he was strapped to his radio room chair. Other than Williams and Baake, everyone else was lost at sea. In memory of the tragedy, the Texas Tower Association has met every year, and Don Abbott heads that association.

That night, the lives of real men with wives and children at home were sent to oblivion. I had forgotten all about it until the exchange with Don Abbott made me realize that these were not just statistics, but people with families, people who had lost their lives because of the advice of experts.

In the investment world, there are hundreds of stock market letters offering advice on what and when to buy or sell. Many knowledgeable men and women write the majority of these letters. The successful writers have large followings and make a lot of money selling their advice.

It seems logical to me that if you pay someone for advice, that person should be an expert. The problem is, there are no experts who can predict what will happen in the stock market. It is probably a good idea to carefully review what experts have stated in other walks of life as well. Yale economist Irving Fisher said before Black Tuesday in 1929, "Stocks are now at what looks like a permanently high plateau," a perfect example of an expert making a classic miscalculation. The British statesman Neville Chamberlain, upon his return from Munich, waved a document and shouted, "I bring you peace in our time."

Market letter writers try to predict the stock market, but it really is impossible to do this. The best writers are right more than they are wrong (barely), but their predictions are not consistent. There are simply too many variables for the human mind to process. There are too many external events—over which we have no control—that affect the stock market. I understand this and now, hopefully, you do as well.

The real question is Can you make money following market letter writers consistently over a long period? Once again, I turn to our friend Vilfredo Pareto. It is safe to say that the majority of market advisors do not make money for their clients over the long run. Predicting the stock market is much more difficult than running a traditional business.

Assuming only 20 percent of all stock market letter writers will make money for their clients over the long haul while 80 percent will be consistent losers, you have a choice to make. Whom will you follow? In my opinion, it makes a lot more sense to identify what the losers, or majority, are telling their clients, rather than try to find those precious few who really know. Fortunately, monitoring the majority is easy to do. I discuss how to monitor this group, along with my entire strategy, in a later chapter.

The media, especially television, is another major obstacle to making money in the stock market. The most popular stock market television station these days is CNBC. It is important to understand why CNBC exists. Is the owner, General Electric, trying to help us make money because they are concerned for our welfare, or are they simply trying to run a successful company? CNBC is a business just like any other enterprise. It has a sales force (reporters), it has revenue (advertising), and it has expenses (salaries). General Electric wants a good return on their investment and the celebrity reporters on CNBC want to keep their jobs. Both groups need viewers, and the best way to get them is to report endlessly about the stock market, constantly looking for provocative issues to discuss.

Unfortunately, most of the market analysts they feature are part of Pareto's Trivial Many. The Vital Few generally do not need to promote themselves and are too busy to take time to appear on television.

It is important to note that I have not advised you to stop reading what experts are saying or to stop watching financial television programs such as CNBC. Quite to the contrary; I want you to pay attention to financial media, but change the way you view them. Instead of looking for investment ideas, I recommend you look for clues or a common theme to what they are advising, and then you can do the opposite.

For example, in May 2002, I noticed that insiders were selling small and mid-sized companies at record rates. This was not surprising because while the Dow Jones Average was struggling, these smaller companies were making new highs. I was thinking about when I would advise my institutional clients to sell these stocks. A few minutes later, I saw two money managers on CNBC talking about how well they were doing. I could not help but notice their lack of humility. It seemed they believed they were solely responsible for their success and did not allow for the fact that they were in a favorable trend for their style of investing.

Using the clue that I had received from CNBC's interview with these portfolio managers, I sent a letter to my clients advising they sell their smaller and mid-sized stocks. It was perfect; The Trivial Many were advising the public to buy and The Vital Few were selling. Three months later, these stocks were pummeled by the market, many losing more than 50 percent of their value.

Another example of how to respond to the media took place in 1984. At that time, I was a stockbroker with Oppenheimer & Company in Fort Lauderdale, Florida. Since 1978, I had hosted a weekly 30-minute television show, *The Muzea Insider Report*, which aired every Monday afternoon. I usually worked on my text over the weekend, but when I arrived in my office one morning the title of the *Wall Street Journal*'s Abreast of the Street column caught my eye: "Oil Prices Surge to $40 a Barrel—Analysts See No Negatives." The article went on to state how most oil analysts expected the price of oil to continue to move dramatically higher. Why this article was so interesting to me was not that it made me want to buy energy stocks, but it was an important clue that we were nearing a top in oil and gas issues.

Before reading the article, I had heard about several dentists in Fort Lauderdale who had sold their practices to move to Houston to search for oil and gas. I also noticed that many of the stockbrokers who had made a lot of money the previous four years in energy stocks were boasting. Since I was following insiders for a living, I could not help but notice that they were selling rather aggressively.

That afternoon on my television show, I pointed out that insiders were selling energy stocks at the same time the public was being advised to buy them. I quoted from the article in the *Wall Street Journal*, which mentioned no negatives. I told my viewers a story about a businessman who looked out of his office window and asked his accountant if he had ever seen business this good. The accountant acknowledged that business was better than ever. With that, the man turned to his accountant and said, "Good, call my broker and sell all of my stocks."

If there truly were no negatives to a further rise in oil prices, then everyone who believed that must already have acted, and that would mean prices of energy stocks would go down because no one would be left to buy them. This is called the Law of Reciprocal Expectations.

The next morning, I called my clients and advised them to sell energy stocks. Most of them did because they knew my theories of contrary or divergent behavior and had profited from them in the past. Unfortunately, some of my newer clients were still ingrained in their old ways—accepting what they saw on television—and did not yet know how to correctly use the media and market experts who made their living advising the public. They learned the hard way. Oil never went higher than on the afternoon of that *Wall Street Journal* article. The news became published at the very top, just prior to a long descent over the next few years.

One of the best examples of The Vital Few and The Trivial Many occurred during the passage of a New Jersey referendum in 1976, which approved gaming in Atlantic City. A year earlier, I had played in a tennis tournament in Hollywood, Florida. My opponent was Mark Cohen, an operating manager for Resorts International, a casino company based in the Bahamas.

After our match, Mark and I had a drink in the clubhouse. We exchanged backgrounds and he seemed quite interested in the fact that I was a stockbroker. Mark said, "We need to talk privately." So we drove to the hotel where he was staying and Mark took a stack of currency from his suitcase. "It's hard getting money out of the islands," he said. "I want you to take this and buy 2,000 shares of Resorts International stock on margin. I believe it's trading at 9½." He handed me $10,000.

When you buy on margin you are betting that the money you are borrowing will bring in more than the interest you will pay the brokerage firm that is lending you the money. For every dollar you invest, the broker will lend you a dollar. This doubles your investment, but also increases your risk.

"On margin?" I asked. "You want to invest two dollars for every dollar you put up?"

"Absolutely," he said.

"Why?"

"We think the State of New Jersey is going to legalize casino gambling in Atlantic City. Nothing has been approved yet, but we're betting it's going to happen and that we will be the first casino to get a license." He then asked, "By the way, what's a short sale?"

"That's when you sell stock you don't own, planning to buy it back later," I explained.

"I have been told that a hedge fund money manager named Bob Wilson is short 350,000 shares of Resorts stock. I heard he was stubborn, and many of our top managers are planning to hold until Wilson buys back."

"Very interesting," I said.

I bought the stock for him and started getting calls from dealers, croupiers, and pit bosses at the Resorts Casino in Paradise Island. Many of them watched my weekly television program. Resorts got the license they needed to open a casino in Atlantic City, and people started lining up for blocks to gamble. Over the next two years, Resorts stock went from $9½ to more than $300 a share!

Almost two years to the day from when Mark and the other employees of Resorts bought, Walter Cronkite put the spotlight on instant millionaires who had made a fortune by investing in Resorts International stock. The week his story ran, the stock hit $300, up $100 during that week alone. I saw elderly couples walking across the street from the Galt Ocean Mile condominiums toward my office carrying their utility stock certificates and asking to trade them in for shares in Resorts International. They were selling conservative stock for a speculative gaming issue based on a spike in price triggered by a national news story.

Bob Wilson could not take the pain of seeing his hedge fund lose millions of dollars, so he took off for London. He bought back (covered) his 350,000-share short position the same week of Cronkite's show, the main reason Resorts went from $200 to $300. Mark and the other Resorts International employees sold into that week's rally.

I told the other brokers in the office not to let their clients buy Resorts stock and instead to recommend electric utilities because my insider analysis indicated I should buy utilities and sell gaming stocks. Most of them ignored me.

The people who bought Resorts International and other gaming stocks that week were selling their utilities stock at the lowest prices in 10 years to buy the very top of gaming stocks. By the end of 1981, the market had gone down 25 percent. Electric utilities was the only group up.

Two years later, Resorts International stock was back to $10. It was the Pareto Principle, the 80:20 Rule, at work again. The Trivial Many had bought the gaming stocks right at the top and had sold their electric utilities at the bottom while The Vital Few had sold into the gaming buys and had bought at the bottom in utilities.

There are countless other examples of how the media can lead you to disaster but also how the more astute use of the media can help you make excellent choices. The key is to analyze what you are reading or seeing in the media and compare it to what you observe yourself. It is also essential that you know what insiders, the most informed investors, are doing. In this way, the media and market letter writers are a true asset. Frankly, I am thrilled that CNBC and their competitors are so popular. They are among the greatest mediums in the world for observing The Trivial Many.

CHAPTER 4

Solution to Mistake #3: Know When the Odds of Investment Success Are in Your Favor

unabashed "market timers" have devised systems to help them anticipate and avoid some of the worst market plunges, protecting their capital by staying in cash through the bad times. Some of these systems are fairly simple to follow, and involve just a few trades a year in index funds. Here, then, are unconventional timing techniques that could help you stay out of the market at most of the worst times and get back in so you benefit from most up ticks. These are not fail-proof, and they cannot predict the market's future direction. But they might help you make better investment decisions. If you want to use them, you should use exchange-traded index funds, which allow you to trade as often as you like, unlike mutual funds. Just be sure to go through a discount broker to minimize fees.

Minimize bear-market damage: Buy-and-hold investing is often cited as the best way to achieve long-term wealth. Indeed, it is a good strategy that produces solid returns over time. But there are two problems. Sure, the market does fully recover over time. The losses suffered by those sticking it out to the bitter end of a bear market, however, can take ages to recoup. The NASDAQ Composite has made an impressive 84% comeback since its bear-market low on October 9, 2002. Yet the index is still 59% below its level in March 2000. The other problem is that many investors who consider themselves buy-and-hold types are nothing of the kind. According to a 2002 survey by the Investment Company Institute and the Securities Industry Association, 86% of individual investors say they practice buy and hold. Yet consulting firm Dalbar found that between 1984 and 2002, equity mutual-fund investors held their funds for an average of 2½ years and got an annual return of 2.6%, well below the 12.2% return for the Standard & Poor's 500 stock index in the same period, and even below inflation. This is not buy-and-hold investing. Instead, it is "buy high, sell low" investing. So given that most of us do in fact try to time the markets in our own way, and that so many of us are doing such a bad job of it, why not use a system that at least has a better track record?

Watch the calendar: You can often beat buy-and-hold by using an indicator as simple as a calendar. Since 1950, the Dow has returned 12.9% annually for the six months between November and April, compared with 4.4% between May and October and 7.7% for the year as a whole, according to Leslie Masonson, author of *All About Market Timing.* So simply buying an index fund November 1 and then transferring to cash on April 30 can improve your returns while reducing risk by keeping you out of the market for half the year. You would have missed, for example, the stock market crash of October 19, 1987, the 1,370-point drop in the Dow in September 2001, and the 1,651-point decline in the third quarter of 2002. On the other hand, you would also have missed the stock market gains of last summer. No system works all the time. But over the long run, the record is impressive.

Follow the election cycle: Presidents tend to give a boost to the economy in the second half of their first term, just in time for their re-election bids. So markets tend to languish in the first couple of years, shoot up in the third year, and be fairly strong in the election year. Between 1901 and 2003, the Dow gained on average 12.5% in pre-election years,

9.3% in election years, 5.2% in post-election years, and 3.2% in midterm years. The Bush administration has so far been a textbook case: losses in the first two years, and a big gain in the pre-election year.

Try a technical approach: For those who are willing to dabble in more complex strategies, the best approach may be to look for professional help. When evaluating different market-timing firms, be wary of outrageous claims—nobody can predict the market or guarantee future returns. And check long-term track records—real-world results count for a lot more than back-tested data. But you don't need an advanced economic degree to use some technical strategies. One option, for example, is to use moving averages. The 200-day moving average simply means the average level of the index over the past 200 days. It is a more long-term measure of the direction of the market than its price on any given day. So market timers often see an index crossing its moving average to the upside as a buy signal, and crossing to the downside as a sell signal. Using shorter periods, such as a 50-day or 20-day moving average, can give quicker indications of when the market is turning, but also are more volatile and so can be harder to read.

Take a seasonal view: You can combine different systems to get the best results. Sy Harding, publisher of the newsletter *Street Smart Report*, has refined the "best six months" strategy by using an indicator based on moving averages to provide a more exact buy or sell signal. He noticed that favorable periods for stocks lasted between four months and eight months, and so he either stretches or limits his investment season depending on the MACD, or moving average convergence divergence.

The key in all of this is to do your research and choose a system you feel comfortable with. Check out free charting services to see how the system would have worked in the past. Then you could maybe try it with a small portion of your savings first, to see how it works in the future. Don't shy away if the system seems to tell you the opposite of what all the experts are saying. As good contrarian investors know, the best time to buy usually is when the herd is screaming, "Sell!"

The preceding article is well written and succinct. Clearly, your ability to make money in the stock market is in direct proportion to your ability to invest only when the odds are with you. In other words, when in doubt, stay out.

I remember, when I was a stockbroker, having a client who was a professional horseracing gambler. I always tried to get to know my biggest clients personally and since he had a seven-figure account with me, I invited him to a dinner party at my house. After dinner, I suggested we go to the racetrack. He agreed but cautioned me that I might be disappointed. I did not ask what he meant, but I soon found out. The following Saturday we were at Calder Racetrack in Miami, Florida. I bet every race, and of course, lost. My client however never made a bet. I asked him how he could just sit and watch the races without betting. He told me that he would never bet on a race unless he liked a horse and the odds to win were at least 3 to 1. All the horses he liked were at lesser odds so he passed. I was amazed and yet somewhat ashamed that I did not have his discipline.

The following weekend, he made four bets (out of nine possible) and won three, giving him a substantial return on his money.

Many racetrack old-timers have said, "You can beat a race, but you can't beat the races." I strongly believe it is the same for the stock market. You can win in the stock market, but if you are always invested, the next bear market can wipe you out. Clearly, you need to consider some use of timing. Making your bets or investments at certain times when the odds are in your favor makes a lot of sense to me and I hope to you as well.

When is it a good time to invest in the stock market? To answer that question, we need to understand some dynamics that pertain to the stock market at various times of the year.

Timing the Stock Market for Success

First Quarter

- *401(k) investments*—401(k) pension plans and IRA investments must be made before April 15 of each year; otherwise the IRS will disallow them. Since the tax year ends on December 31 for individuals, most of their money flows into these plans in the first quarter of each year. A large percentage are invested in public mutual funds, such as those owned and run by Fidelity Investments and Alliance Capital.
- *Public mutual funds*—Most money managers of public mutual funds have to be fully invested at all times. This is due to the popularity of fund of funds managers who raise money for mutual funds but insist that they be fully in-

vested. Fund of funds managers diversify and spread risk by putting money into various mutual funds that have differing investment styles. Since most mutual fund money managers have to be fully invested at all times, 401(k) and IRA money put into mutual funds forces these money managers to buy stocks until the money inflows dry up.

It makes sense to avoid buying into the demand for stocks created by the huge sums of money invested in IRAs and 401(k)s in the first quarter. When this flow of money is fully invested, usually by the end of April, the market usually drops as demand dries up.

Fourth Quarter

- *Institutional tax loss selling*—Individuals have until December 31 of each year to offset losses with gains. Many investors are unaware that the mutual fund industry must balance gains and losses by October 31 of each year. This creates an artificial supply for stocks in the September–October period each year as the mutual fund money managers sell their losers to offset capital gains they had during the year.

Clearly, you will have a better probability of success in buying stocks in the fourth quarter of each year as sell-offs occur for reasons other than the company's fundamentals. When the institutional tax loss selling ends on October 31, the stock market will usually rise, as the pressure on many stocks is gone.

Let us look at some facts. Since 1957, 57 percent of all market tops have occurred in February–April and 77 percent of all bottoms took place in October–December. In 1986, when the mutual fund industry's tax year changed to October 31, cycle predictability got even better. Since 1986, 67 percent of all market tops have occurred in the first quarter and 86 percent of all market bottoms took place in October–December. Clearly, if you were to focus on buy programs in the fourth quarter each year, your chances for success would improve dramatically.

We now have all the pieces necessary to become consistent winners in the stock market. We have a strategy. We know whom to follow and not follow, and we know that there are certain times to invest that have a higher probability for success than others.

It is now time to talk about insider trading. After all, insiders are The Vital Few, and we need to understand the rules governing their behavior, how to use them, and where to go to get an accurate assessment of what they are doing in the stock market at any given time. It is also useful for me to discuss some of my experiences, how they led me to discover the value of insider behavior, and my thought process as to how I developed my ideas for using the media to my advantage.

CHAPTER 5

Insiders, The Vital Few

THE SECURITIES AND EXCHANGE COMMISSION (SEC) HAS DEEMED OF-
ficers and directors of publicly traded companies as corporate
insiders. Individuals who are outsiders but have managed to
accumulate 10 percent or more of a publicly traded stock are
also insiders.

The rules governing insider trading are clear and straightforward. Any change in holdings by an insider must be reported to
the SEC within two business days of the transaction. Insiders are
allowed to trade whenever they want; However, if it can be
proved they took advantage of information that was not available
to the public, they can be forced to turn their profits back to the
company and be sued for treble damages in civil court.

Under the Freedom of Information Act, the SEC is required to
make this information available to the public. There are many
ways to find out what stocks insiders are buying or selling, but

before I discuss how to get the information, it is important that you understand how to use it.

The key word that you will read many times in this book is "divergence." Normal insider behavior would be to buy into price weakness and to sell into price strength. Just because they are corporate insiders does not necessarily mean they are savvy investors. A minority of insiders, mostly those with Wall Street roots, understand the investment community's response to news and are very conscious of the future trend of earnings and other important developments they expect to report. The majority of insiders, however, do not have a clue as to what causes their companies' stock prices to go up or down. This group is primarily focused on the inherent value of the stock relative to its current price.

Regardless of whether corporate insiders are focused on news they expect to report or comparative values, all insiders understand the intrinsic value of their own companies' stock. Intrinsic value is the price at which a company could be liquidated or sold to an interested buyer. When their company's stock approaches or drops below intrinsic value, insiders buy. The lower it goes, the more they buy. On the other hand, when stock prices rise above their perception of intrinsic value, insiders sell. The higher it goes, the more they sell.

Since it is normal for insiders to buy as their stock goes down and sell as it goes up, what we want to look for are divergences from this normal behavior. Your eyes should become wide open when you see an insider, especially the Chief Financial Officer who normally sells stock only when the price rises, suddenly break this pattern by selling into price weakness. It usually means that the company's business conditions have deteriorated and that bad news is coming. On the other hand, you should really be impressed when you see insiders buy at higher prices than their earlier purchases. This usually means business conditions are at least as strong as they were when these insiders first bought, and in many cases, getting stronger. Better than expected news usually surfaces a few months later.

My firm, Muzea Insider Consulting Services, analyzes insider trading for institutions. We have identified both of the insider groups discussed previously. We call the group that does not care about earnings visibility Value Insiders. These insiders concern themselves only with the book value in relation to their current stock price. Approximately 70 percent of all insiders fall into this category. Investors who are interested in buying stocks that have suffered declines and seem to be at attractive price levels should monitor the trading of Value Insiders. If a stock has real value at depressed levels and Value Insiders are not buying, use that as an alert to rethink your own assessment of value in the stock in question. On the other hand, insider buying would give you added confidence that your reasoning is sound and you can begin your accumulation without reservation. From a macro, or big picture, perspective it is important to know what Value Insiders are doing as a group. If the market has experienced a decline and they have not bought aggressively, clearly the decline has more to go. In my 37 years of following insiders, I have never seen an intermediate or major stock market bottom without aggressive accumulation of stocks in general by Value Insiders.

The second group my company has identified is Catalytic Insiders. These insiders do not care about book value. Their main concern is with visibility and will buy only if they see good news over the next two quarters. If you are interested in buying a stock that is already in a clearly defined up trend, the actions of the Catalytic Insiders can be helpful. The investment community has labeled investors who buy stocks that are only in established up trends as momentum investors. Since these investors buy only stocks that are well off their lows and already have experienced a surge in prices and breakouts from bases, the risk is greater for this class of investor. At some point in time, there will be a final breakout in price that becomes the top for that cycle. The challenge for momentum investors is to not get caught in that last breakout in the price of their stock. Monitoring the actions of Catalytic Insiders can be helpful in this regard. If this group of insiders have bought the most recent basing pattern (a period of lateral price movement), it is highly likely that more good news is on its way and the subsequent surge in prices will not be a head fake. If, on the other hand, insiders who previously bought are not buying the new basing pattern, it would be wise for a momentum investor to not buy the next breakout of a base and to either sell into the new rally or at least place stops to protect their gains.

From a macro point of view, monitoring both groups of insiders can be very useful in determining the degree of market risk at any given time. In an ideal world, Value Insiders provide us with a clue that the stock market has exceptional value. Then when Catalytic Insiders buy, that would be a sign that the turn is near.

It is logical for the Value Insiders to come in first, but it is also possible that both groups both buy at the same time. This usually happens after a sharp market drop, such as what happened in October/November 1987. I have never seen a secular bull market that did not have both Value and Catalytic Insiders buying. Therefore, it is important to monitor their behavior. Since it is normal for Value Insiders to buy first, the major clue we get as to whether the ensuing rally is going to become only a trading event or the start of a new major up trend will be the actions of the Catalytic Insiders. On the other hand, if the Catalytic Insiders buy aggressively, then we can look for a major move in the economy, company profits, and the stock market. We would know the market is undervalued from the actions of the Value Insiders and when the buying of the Catalytic Insiders confirms that, the next up move is significant. Absent Catalytic Insider buying would indicate only a technical rally. The stock market could then be expected to drop back again to the previous level or close to it. Without Catalytic Insider buying, there will not be enough good news from companies to keep stocks moving higher.

It is quite easy to identify both groups of insiders. Value Insiders buy only stocks that are at either the bottom one-third of their 52-week price range or at intermediate lows. The key to understanding Value Insider behavior is that they are looking for bargain prices in their company's stock. They are very patient and if you are going to follow them, you better have that quality as well. Otherwise, you might give up in disgust and sell just before the stock gets recognized and starts its up trend.

The Catalytic Insider is also easy to follow. In my company, we have identified this group as Stud Insiders and Smart Insiders. However, you do not need the names of these insiders. Anytime you see an insider buying a stock that is already in an up trend, the insider buying is "catalytic" in nature. Any insider buying into price strength is good. However, if the buying is coming from operating officers, the probability of good news coming is further enhanced. There is nothing better that having one or more insiders buying into a stock that is in an up trend and already has institutional sponsorship. The good news often leads to institutional research analysts' upgrades, which often precede additional spikes in prices. The Catalytic Insider is actually the momentum investor's best friend.

It is important to understand that insiders really have only about a six-month visibility on their company's prospects. They have a good handle on business conditions for about two quarters. However, beyond that they are guessing just like everyone else. I am amused when I read analyst reports basing price objectives on predicted earnings two years out.

Understanding that insider visibility is only about six months, it is important to keep monitoring their activity in stocks you own. For example, you like a stock, it has insider buying, so you buy it. Six months later, the stock has moved up 25 percent and you observe there is additional insider buying. Great! That is a sign that more good news is coming and the stock probably has good prospects for the next six months.

On the other hand, what would you do if the stock had moved ahead sharply, six months elapse, and there is no further insider buying or even some profit taking? A stock like this should be monitored carefully for signs of weakness. As long as the stock maintains its up trend, I would stay with it, but if it starts to stagger a bit, I would sell.

A wise old successful investor told me years ago that one of his best methods of knowing when to sell was the actions of the stocks in his own portfolio. As the market would rise and he found new stocks to buy, he would pause when his next stop failed to go up. He would then buy another stock. If that one failed to go up or went down, he would sell all of his stocks. This may seem a bit extreme, but I do believe the action of your own portfolio of stocks can help you know when to sell. Knowing whether insiders did or did not buy more after their initial six-month entry point can be very helpful in this regard.

There are many Internet web sites that allow you to check for insider trading in a stock. I recommend Yahoo!, which has a Finance option that allows you to select the insider option after you have entered a symbol. It is also free, and does a good job of presenting the insider data. I recommend you ignore everything except open market buying and selling. Any insider trades other than simple open market trading is too complicated and not worth the time required to analyze.

It is also very useful to know the biography of insiders who are trading in a stock of your interest. When you are in Yahoo! Finance, select the Profile link and then select the option that provides you with the full list of insiders. Knowing how long an insider has been with the company, when he or she last traded, and what their position is could provide you with valuable clues as to just how important the trade is.

Macro analysis is a top-down approach that consists of mainly two areas. The first is the determination of the degree of market risk or reward that exists at any given time in the market. The second is the analysis of sectors and industries. Many of my company's institutional clients are interested in clues about which sectors and industries corporate insiders favor or disfavor. Over the years, we have developed a number of proprietary techniques that aggregate all insider trading, and we have years of back data to compare.

It is next to impossible for the average individual investor to duplicate the insider data that my firm has compiled over the past 25 years. Without back data, it is better not to attempt the analysis of insider trading to predict sectors and industries. Do not fret, however. Remember, 60 percent of your investing success is a function of knowing the risk/reward of the market at any given time. You will have that problem solved with the Magic T described in a later chapter.

Twenty percent of your investing success relates to stock selection. This, too, is in the bag since you now have a method of checking insider trading in your stock, which should improve overall results when insiders and your own analysis are in synch.

The last 20 percent of successful investing is checking the sector and industry where your stock resides. A smart way to gain insights here without quitting your full-time job (I am not sure that would help anyway) is to pay attention to your own reading and research. When you develop an interest in a sector or industry, write down the market leaders on a piece of paper, and check out the insider trading in these stocks. The existence or lack of insider buying will give you a good clue as to whether there is overall value.

The best way, however, to gain sector and industry insights is to simply focus on the stocks you have already identified as buy candidates. You did your research and checked out the insider trading. Now all you have to do is get a list of other companies that are in the same sector and industry and check out their insider trading profiles. If you see similar insider buying, then you have an excellent confirmation that the stock you already like is more than just a special situation. If other companies in the same sector and industry also have good insider buying patterns, you now have that final 20 percent working in your favor.

If the preceding seems like a lot of work, it is. Remember though, you are rewarded in life and in the stock market by what you ferret out yourself. Useful information is rarely given out for free; it has to be dug out. Information that comes easily, such as viewing financial media and buying a 50-cent newspaper is relatively useless, designed for the masses or The Trivial Many.

I would like to make one final point. The concept of avoiding or selling any stock that has insider selling into price weakness is the most important lesson you can learn when it comes to following insiders. Investors could have saved enormous amounts of money over the years if they had simply followed this one, single insider analysis rule. If you learn nothing but this one insider concept from my book, I would be very pleased and gratified because I know I have taught you a technique that can help you avoid major losses in a declining stock. Avoiding big losers is even more important than picking winners, in my opinion, because losses not only destroy hard-earned stock market gains but have an emotional cost as well.

CHAPTER 6

Divergence Is the Key to Following The Vital Few

I DID NOT JUST WAKE UP ONE MORNING AND DECIDE THAT LOOKING for divergences in insider behavior was going to make me rich. I became wealthy over the years by perfecting my methodology of following insiders. Actually, my understanding of divergent behavior and its relevance to many walks of life started in my youth.

I was born in Webster, Massachusetts, and lived there for the first 18 years of my life. My main love in high school was football. My team played in the Central Massachusetts Class 2 Division against schools much larger and better funded than ours such as Worcester South, Auburn, and Mary E. Wells of neighboring Southbridge.

The rivalry between my school, Bartlett, and Mary E. Wells had started back in 1906 and by the time I came along, it was so intense that no one would go to the other town for any reason if we could help it, even during the off-season.

In my senior year, I was co-captain and played starting quarterback. We were undefeated that year going into the annual Thanksgiving game in Southbridge. Wells had only one loss, so the winner would claim the division championship and bragging rights for the year.

The last undefeated Bartlett team had won in 1925. It was our chance to do it again, and we were powered up. I knew Wells had been looking us over, and I had had a chance to watch them play as well. One of the things I noticed was that whenever the opposing team moved its fullback to one side of the playing field, Wells would shift their defense to that side. This made it tough to run against a stacked defense. I also knew that when our offense placed our fullback to the right or to the left, we always ran or passed to that side.

"Coach," I asked, "can I talk to you about a strategy I think could win this game for us?"

"Sure."

"I've been watching Wells, and it seems they tend to overshift their defense to the fullback's side. We need a reverse move of some kind to throw them off."

"You're right," the coach said, "but that means you will have to run with the ball. I have been thinking about this, but we would be in trouble if you got hurt."

I must have looked disappointed because he immediately said, "Since this is our last game, tell you what, let's run a play or two where you roll out to the opposite side of our fullback. Then you can run or pass, depending on what happens with their defense."

"Got it."

"One thing, George, don't do these rollouts too early in the game, or they'll be onto us and adjust their defense."

"Okay."

The Thanksgiving game played on a beautiful day to a packed crowd of 6,000 fans. As expected, Wells shut our offense down the first half. With a minute left, we were down 12–0 and we had the ball on their 45-yard line. I figured the time was right and called a rollout to the right. I put our fullback, Pete Teguis, flanked out to the left. On this play, everyone was to run toward Teguis, except our two tight ends. One end would run straight and cross over to the right deep into the field. The other end would go to the right, about 15 yards in front of the other player. Then I would roll to the right.

It worked like a charm. Both ends were wide open. I lofted the ball to the tight end closest to me. He pulled the ball out of the sky and rumbled into the end zone untouched. With the extra point we began the second half 12–7.

Wells did not know what had happened, and we kept up our divergent strategy. I threw two more touchdown passes and even ran for one. We won the game 34–12 and went on to take the state championship.

Recently, I met a man who played for Mary E. Wells in that game. He told me that for years he had thought about that game and had asked himself many times why his team had collapsed in the second half. When I told him about our divergent strategy, he thanked me. I guess I eased his pain.

The practice of looking at abrupt changes in behavior patterns to alert you to impending problems can save you serious money, if you apply it to your business relationships. In the mid-1980s, I was a stockbroker with Drexel Burnham in Fort Lauderdale, Florida. I was asked on several occasions to participate in a question-and-answer show about the stock market on national television. Filming was in Los Angeles and the studio put me up at the Beverly Wilshire Hotel, directly opposite Rodeo Drive and across from Drexel's office. Michael Milken owned the building and leased it to Drexel. During my third trip to L.A., I noticed that the company's name had been removed from the building. I believed the absence of Drexel Burnham's name was divergent behavior, and a sign of Milken's arrogance. In my opinion, he was telling Drexel that if they did not like what he was doing, then he would put another name on the building—Shearson, Milken or whatever. I resigned from my position at Drexel Burnham the next morning. One week later, a federal government grand jury indicted Milken and other Drexel officers for insider trading violations and other market manipulations. I was one of the few employee stockholders to get out with the bulk of my cash when a couple of years later the company was forced into bankruptcy.

Years earlier, I was a stockbroker with E.F. Hutton in Pompano Beach, Florida. I knew quite a bit about tax shelters for high net worth individuals, so I decided to watch for new offerings in this area. In the mid-1970s, ordinary income was taxed at 50 percent, while dividends and interest were taxed at 70 percent. At that time, the U.S. government approved tax shelters for investors in order to encourage domestic oil and gas exploration. Generally, these programs offered oil and gas programs that promised a 5-for-1-tax write-off and a good chance of doubling the capital invested. For example, you could invest $10,000 and receive $50,000 in tax deductions. Even if you got only your principal back, it was a good deal because of the tax savings. Of course, there still was some risk.

In 1975, Tesoro Petroleum offered an oil and gas tax shelter program that seemed to push the limits of reality. My firm was the investment banker and sponsor, and we told our brokers that it could give a 10-to-1 return. Our commission was $800 for each $10,000 invested, a good incentive to market the product. The day before I started calling leads, I saw an insider filing revealing that one of Hutton's senior officers had sold a substantial amount of Tesoro stock.

I viewed the sale as a divergence from normal behavior. I expected a senior officer of the firm in a high tax bracket to buy the offering and take advantage of the 5–1 write-off, so I decided against offering the tax shelter to my clients. The Tesoro tax shelter program was a disaster because one of their oil refining plants in Puerto Rico had major problems. The 10-for-1 return was reversed. Instead of a huge profit, the deal gave investors only ten cents back for each dollar invested.

This fueled my interest in following and analyzing insider behavior. Perhaps the Hutton officer did not know that Tesoro was in trouble, but I found it very interesting that a few years later he donated $15 million to the Harvard Business School to establish a course in business ethics. Somewhere I read that the president of the business school said the gift was unusual, and I remember thinking, "Could this be his penance?" We will never know.

Maybe he was just lucky. More important, however, I learned that I could follow what insiders did and ignore what they said if their actions did not support their words.

Most of my investment career was built on the simple strategy of watching for divergences, a valuable business tool learned on the playing fields as a teenager involved in competitive sports.

CHAPTER 7

Examples of
The Vital Few
versus
The Trivial Many

IN 1988, I WAS WORKING AS DIRECTOR OF RESEARCH FOR INVEST/NET Corporation, a South Florida company that held the SEC contract to process insider filings. One of my responsibilities was to write a weekly newsletter to institutional clients advising them of any interesting insider buying.

By this time, I was thoroughly indoctrinated into Pareto's 80:20 Rule and totally engrossed in analyzing insider behavior. I had also trained myself to view the media as a contrary indicator.

In the spring of 1988, I recommended Columbia Pictures (KPE) to our clients because the insider filings revealed that Dan Lufkin, founder of Donaldson, Lufkin and Jenrette, and Charlie Allen, co-founder of Los Angeles investment company Allen and Company, were buying large blocks of the stock at $7. Lufkin was on the board of Columbia Pictures, and Allen was on the board of Sony Corporation.

I thought these insiders were well schooled in the ways of Wall Street's response to news, and there was a possibility that good news was coming. When I read in *Barron's* magazine that Goldman Sachs was recommending KPE as a short sale to its hedge funds, I became even more interested.

Goldman believed the company had no decent films on the horizon, a bad balance sheet, and an incompetent creative director, but I begged to differ since Lufkin was on Columbia's board, and it was quite possible that the research from Goldman was flawed.

A few weeks after my recommendation, Columbia's stock rose to the $9 area as rumors circulated that it was a takeover candidate. At the same time, I observed that analysts on popular investment television programs were adamant that there was no deal in the future—Dan Dorfman being the most strident. This famous (and infamous) market commentator, with his trademark squeaky voice, was the highest paid financial journalist in the world as well as one of the most influential. At his zenith, his remarks carried such influence that the Chicago Board Options Exchange instituted a rule just because of him, which they called the Dorfman Rule. His opinions carried so much weight that the Exchange actually would temporarily halt trading options of stocks he mentioned in his broadcasts. Dorfman often broke news in his columns, including some of the largest mergers and contested takeovers at that time.

His negative comments brought the stock back to $7. I recall watching the show as he pointed his finger at the television camera and almost hyperventilated, "I can tell you with great certainty that there is no deal in the making for Columbia Pictures."

A few weeks later, I saw insider filings that both Lufkin and Allen had bought more stock into the price dip. Dorfman had incited The Trivial Many to sell, while The Vital Few (including some of my followers) continued to buy. I reiterated my recommendation to my institutional clients.

Ten months later, Sony made a cash buyout offer for $27.50 per share. Allen and Company handled the negotiations, making millions in investment banking fees, while Charlie Allen and Dan Lufkin loaded millions of dollars in trading profits into their personal accounts.

In the late 1980s, the SEC prosecuted Ivan Boesky and Michael Milken for insider trading violations, and Boesky was the first stock trader to pay a fine of $100 million. Both went to jail. Milken's $600 million penalty left him with only about a billion dollars, while Boesky completed his truncated jail term in 1990 with $100 million left in cash.

It seems to me the prosecution of Boesky and Milken is another example of the futility of insider trading rules. The SEC catches only the big fish, the tip of the iceberg, while every day violations occur that the government has neither the manpower nor the will to prosecute. It was that way in 1988, and I believe it will always be that way.

I left Invest/Net after Thomson Financial Services had bought them in 1994. Thomson seemed more interested in marketing than in pure research. We also disagreed in our approaches to working with institutional investors. My approach was simply to provide the best insider research available and constantly work to improve my product. I completely believed in the proverb "If you build a better mousetrap, the world will beat a path to your door."

After leaving Invest/Net, my wife Maria I started our own consulting firm with only two accounts, each managing between \$150–\$200 million dollars. At the beginning of 2002, eight years later, Muzea Insider Consulting Services consisted of 7 employees advising 60 money management firms in the U.S. and Europe, totaling approximately \$1 trillion dollars under management. This was accomplished without having a full sales force, vindicating my better mousetrap theory.

I was especially pleased when we signed on a very successful hedge fund, the Quantum Fund, run by George Soros and Stanley Druckenmiller. *Institutional Investor* magazine hailed Soros as "the world's greatest money manager." In 1992, Soros and Druckenmiller risked \$10 billion that the British pound would fall. Their instincts were right and the Quantum Fund's profit was almost \$2 billion. This earned them international notoriety and guru status among traders.

I had developed a niche business that would fall within the realm of nontraditional Wall Street research, which is typically obscure. The people who operate this type of business usually work out of a small office and are often quite independent. They are free from the pressure that traditional Wall Street research analysts get from their investment banking departments. It is difficult to be objective when you know your firm will lose millions of dollars of underwriting fees if you publish a negative research report. Nontraditional research firms face none of this pressure. I observed how difficult it was for many professionals to stay disciplined when I worked in the investment business in New York and Boston. Rumors circulated daily and opinions flew readily from all sources.

When new clients ask me, "Why do you live in Reno, Nevada?"

I tell them about the fantastic quality of life here and add, "Besides, I like operating in relative obscurity in a small mining town in the West."

The demise of Enron Corporation, and others too numerous to mention, was the tip of the iceberg for the first decade of the twenty-first century. Enron reminds me of a company in the early 1970s called Equity Funding, a popular institutional stock whose Chief Executive Officer was promoting the growth of the company at analyst meetings and conference calls.

He was selling heavily at the same time he was promoting the stock. As a stockbroker with E.F. Hutton, I had alerted my retail clients telling them to avoid the stock. The company was indeed growing as fast as the CEO told analysts, except they were using fictitious names of new customers. When the whistle blew, the stock was halted from trading at $35 and never reopened.

After that, I always figured I would never find a business fraud comparable to Equity Funding. That was, of course, until Enron. In just 15 years, Enron grew from nothing to America's seventh largest company, employing 21,000 people in more than 40 countries. The firm's success, however, turned out to be nothing more than an elaborate fraud. Enron lied about profits and was accused of a range of shady dealings, including concealing debts so they did not show up in the company's financial statements. What astonished me was the zeal the investment community had for this company. Enron fooled many smart people, but in the end, these executives were no different from some insiders. They are in the category of those who do not back up their words with deeds.

When Enron stock was trading in the mid-80s, I issued a sell signal to my institutional clients and repeated that sell signal again and again over the next 14 months while insiders continued to sell their stock at lower prices, a surefire sign of major problems.

The company went into bankruptcy, and many employees and small investors were hurt. Meanwhile, the media pumped up the Enron story, forcing the SEC to promise insider trading reforms again. This time some changes were made, most notably the requirement that insiders report their trades within two business days, when in the past they had 30 to 45 days to report. Nothing much has changed though. Every day there are small violations that the SEC ignores; the next nationwide scandal is probably in the making right now, just waiting for the whistle to blow. In my opinion, insiders will always take advantage of what they know (greed is a powerful emotion). In spite of all the regulations, their risk of being apprehended is small, even though there are billions of dollars at stake.

One of the more interesting regulations adopted in 2000 was Regulation Full Disclosure (Reg FD). This rule eliminated the practice of selective disclosure. Reg FD requires that when a public company chooses to release any information, it must be done in such a way that the general public has access to it at the same time as institutional investors and analysts. If information is released to specific parties, the company must disseminate that information widely within 24 hours.

Regulation FD underscores the need for companies to be extremely careful in the way they communicate to the investment community any material information that has been nonpublic. Among the measures that many companies take to exercise care

are: (1) limiting in writing the group of persons authorized to speak for the company, (2) making conference calls with analysts readily accessible by the public, (3) preceding the calls with clear announcements of how the calls can be accessed, and (4) encouraging analysts to ask all of their questions during the conference calls, thereby minimizing follow-up calls seeking private advice.

I love Regulation FD! I have always had a disdain for traditional Wall Street research and consider most security analysts simply reporters. Reg FD has dealt the street's good old boy network (a select group of analysts and their followers who received advance material information) a death blow. If you need proof that Reg FD is working, all you have to do is observe how consistently wrong the majority of research analysts are with their quarterly earnings projections. Those few analysts who actually kick tires and spend a lot of time researching companies and analyzing company prospects are finally getting the recognition they deserve.

For those of us who spend our days analyzing insider trading, Reg FD is a bonanza. Our institutional clients use a variety of techniques in picking stocks, and our evaluation of insider trading in stocks on their watch lists has always been important to them. Now, because of lessened reliance on traditional Wall Street research, they are relying even more heavily on our insider research.

Individual investors have gained as well with Regulation FD. In a way, it forces the average investor to do what he or she should have been doing all along—developing their own style of investing and avoiding reliance on others, especially research analysts. If you are going to be a consistent winner in the stock market, you have to do it yourself.

CHAPTER 8

Sharpening Your Ability to Process Investment Information from Print and Television Media

YOUR ABILITY TO BE A CONSISTENT WINNER IN THE STOCK MARKET, and in life for that matter, is in direct proportion to your ability to process information correctly.

As a Naval officer stationed on the aircraft carrier USS *Wasp*, I was part of a crew conducting a routine exercise in the North Atlantic early in 1963. From my position on the bridge, I could see the forward and middle parts of the ship, but not the back where the third elevator was located. One bright spring day in March, two helicopters were getting ready to take off from an area next to the third elevator at the same time a jet fighter was circling the carrier requesting permission to land. Somehow the signals got confused and the air boss, Commander Robert Mead, gave permission for the plane to land at the same moment that the operations officer below deck gave the green light for the helicopters to take off. Neither officer could have foreseen the danger until it was too late, and the jet fighter crashed into one of the helicopters, sending flames from the explosion 100 feet into the sky.

We were steaming into the wind at 20 knots. With the wind blowing about 15 knots, the combined 35 knots made it easier for planes to take off and land. When the accident occurred, the wind was blowing the flames into other planes that were parked on the flight deck. Captain William Brewer immediately ordered the ship to reduce speed and turn out of the wind. I got on the radio and advised the two destroyers who were on either side of the carrier that we were making an emergency turn.

Once we were downwind, the flames subsided and the flight deck crews quickly extinguished them. However, it was too late for the pilot of the jet fighter and the three men in the helicopter.

After this incident, a system of signal lights was put in place. Identical lights were installed on the captain's bridge, the air commander's control location, and the operation officer's station. In addition to three-way communication, all the lights would have to be lit green to launch fixed wing planes or red to launch helicopters. When the captain saw all three lights in unison, he would press a button and the lights would blink, indicating the all-clear signal. This made it impossible for such an accident ever to happen again.

This experience taught me that you have to be aware of your surroundings and pay attention to details. My determination to avoid placing myself in a situation where something could go wrong extended to the stock market. Pareto's 80:20 Rule made a lot of sense to me when I first read it. I knew that my success in helping clients was dependent on my ability to observe whether my thinking was with The Vital Few or The Trivial Many. What I learned about anticipating problems on the bridge of the USS

Wasp, after that tragic accident on the flight deck occurred, was largely responsible for my success as a securities broker.

I also learned several things about being aware and processing information correctly through playing tennis. In the early 1980s, I was ranked 85th in the country in amateur tennis. That year, I was the number two seed playing a tournament in Key Biscayne, Florida. With my record, I was expected to make it to the finals.

Playing in the center court, I was thrilled to see a couple of hundred people in the bleachers. A large crowd was unusual for a first round match.

My opponent was a tall blond whose muscles rippled as he whacked a few balls across the net to loosen up. As I typically did during the warm-up before a match, I hit him various shots, some flat, others with spin, to see how he would handle them. I could tell he was not that great a player because he had good serves and strong returns, but he just did not seem to have his ground stroke technique down.

I served first to start the match. After a couple of exchanges across the net, I noticed he was six or seven feet behind the baseline. My backhand drop shot was deadly, so I leaned in as if I was going to slice my backhand cross court and at the last minute stopped my racquet so that the ball fluttered into the air and landed softly on his side of the court, just on the other side of the net.

I had him good. I stretched out my hand, caught the ball coming my way from across the net, and called out, "Fifteen-love!" Winning the first point was sweet.

"Love-fifteen!" he shouted back to me.

What? What was he talking about? Some of the people watching the game were my friends, and I could hear them laughing along with everyone else. They thought it was hilarious.

"Don't you know?" one of them asked me. "You're playing the world's fastest white man!"

My opponent was a world-class athlete who had won the silver medal in the Olympics in the 100-meter dash. He had closed the space between the back of the court and the net in time to connect with the ball and send it over to me. Only instead of hitting it back, I had caught it, and had lost the point.

In all of my life in finance and sports, I have never been so sure I was right only to be shown seconds later that I was dead wrong.

From then on, I have tried to be a little more careful before assuming anything until all the facts are in. More importantly, I got a fast lesson that day in sizing up other people. I had assumed my opponent was average at best and certainly no match for my skills. Exactly the opposite was the case. I learned with one backhand shot that it is dangerous to assume other people do not have what it takes. Think the best of them, and play your strategy accordingly. Never judge a book by its cover.

The best way to improve your ability to process information from the media is to actively challenge what you are reading or seeing on television. Ask yourself "Why am I getting this information? Who is giving me the input and why now? Does the information jive with what I already know? Is what I am being exposed to popular or is it a minority opinion? Does my knowledge of current insider behavior back the information or refute it? Did I recently hear people talking about this information at a party, and was I impressed with the people who believed in the information?"

The more you practice this kind of interaction with the media, the better you will get, and you will be well on your way to becoming part of The Vital Few.

With any major decision including investments, it helps to use the Magic T, one of the most valuable tools I have ever worked with. Every day, you and I make as many as 50 decisions—what clothes to wear, what to eat, and so on. If you are correct only 50 percent of the time with these small decisions, you are still alright. However, when it comes to major decisions, such as marriage, career change, relocation, or whether to take a major position in the stock market, you must try to make these decisions 100 percent correct.

The Magic T will help you do that. Here is how to create the Magic T. Draw a large *T* on a full-sized sheet of notebook paper. Above the top left column, write one of your two major choices and at the top right, list the other choice. Under each of the two columns, write down five positive outcomes you anticipate from each decision. Now you have 10 positive points for your 2 choices. Identify one of the 10 that is the most important to you and give it a rating of "10." Be brutally honest with yourself, and try to remain totally objective. Rate the second most important positive choice a "9." Continue until all 10 have been rated. Add up the score for each column and you have an objective appraisal telling you the decision you should make. I have used the Magic T dozens of times myself and have taught it in seminars and consultations with many people.

Following is a letter I wrote in January 2004 to my son Marcus, who lives in Holland with his wife and two daughters. It is a good example of the Magic T that I used in the past, and I wanted to share it with my son. He had just turned 42 and was faced with a major decision affecting his life and his family. I sent this letter to help him understand how to make the right choice in the midst of any emotional moments.

Dear Marcus,

About 35 years ago, a wise old man taught me a formula to help me make intelligent long-term decisions. He recognized that in any given day, people make dozens of small decisions such as what to wear, where to eat, and so on. If 50 percent of these decisions are correct, that is normal and the outcome does not really matter. With long-term decisions, however, one needs to be 100 percent correct. These important decisions could be a career change, marriage, buying a home, or relocating. The key to making good long-term choices is one's ability to get emotions out of the decision, something that is very difficult to do. I have used a formula called the Magic T successfully over the years and now I am going to pass it on to you. One day, you can teach it to your daughters. The best way for me to explain the Magic T is to give you two real-life examples of how I used it in the past.

When I was 33, I was manager of a large brokerage firm in Boston. I was in line for a major advancement, but I wasn't happy and the stress caused me to become concerned about my health. A good friend of mine had just died of a heart attack, and my family history of heart disease was hovering in the back of my mind. On the other hand, I was being considered for future top management, and if I turned my back on the firm's long-term plans for me, I could never succeed with them. If I left the company, I would be giving up millions of dollars, prestige, and power. It was a stressful time, but I made the right decision. Using the formula in the Magic T, I made a list of five positive points about each decision (no negatives) and put them into columns. After I had five on each side, I decided which is the most important and assigned that point a 10. The next most important point got a 9, and so forth. After adding up each column, the side with the highest total number was the choice I made.

Florida as a Stockbroker	Boston as a Manager
Less stress (10)	Power, prestige, and money (7)
Healthy lifestyle (9)	Great culture (2)
Year round tennis (8)	Intelligent, sophisticated women to date (6)
Less responsibility, more control (3)	Good friends and familiar surroundings (5)
Live near brother and mother (4)	Skiing at Killington in rented chalet (1)
Totals 34	21

(I made the move to Florida, got everything I wanted, improved my lifestyle, and I'm glad I made this decision.)

The second Magic T was an equally important decision. It concerned two women I was in love with and both loved me. One was an old flame who had come back into my life after I was already involved with another woman. I had asked Joyce to marry me a year earlier and her timing was a cosmic tragedy to me because I had fallen in love with

Maria. I knew I had to make a decision or risk being single the rest of my life, most likely.

Marry Joyce	*Marry Maria*
Very bright and exciting to be with (9)	Very loving and caring (10)
Extremely loyal (6)	Very easy to be with (5)
No baggage, just her (4)	Ready-made family with 3-year-old son (7)
Good sense of humor (3)	Friends and family love her (2)
Great to travel with (1)	Organized and good in business (8)
Totals 23	32

(As you know, I married Maria. It was the right decision, and I am happily married. We built a business together and have many happy memories, many of which you have shared with us.)

I hope this helps and please call me if you want my help with the Magic T.

Best always, and much love,

Dad

Try the Magic T if you are not sure whether to invest in the stock market. At the top of the left column of the T, write Buy and on the right side, write Stay Out.

On a separate sheet of paper list the following factors: Insiders,

Advisory sentiment, Mood of the media, Mood of friends and acquaintances, and State of the stock market. Then place your analysis on the Magic T paper. For example, Insiders are buying would be placed under Buy. Advisory sentiment shows more pessimism than optimism, so place it under Buy. NBC is parading out lots of bearish analysts; put it under Buy. You have observed that many of your friends are frightened, especially those who seem to always make bad decisions; it goes under Buy. Finally, the stock market is depressed and in a downtrend; place this under Buy as well. This would be a low-risk buying opportunity, supported by The Vital Few versus The Trivial Many concept. Other times, Stay Out will be prominent and much of the time there will be a mixed picture. A mixed picture means you have a 50/50 chance of picking winners. You would have to be very careful in what you buy during those times.

Chapter 13 goes into more detail on the Magic T, while Chapter 14 provides you with examples of the Magic T in action.

Irving Kreit, a broker in my office when I worked in Boston, was a big producer and a genial man in his early fifties. One day I said, "What do you think of the market, Irving?" I wanted to see if he and I were in synch. It was the spring of 1970 and I felt the stock market would soon be heading for a sharp decline.

"I'm moving my clients out of stocks and into corporate bonds," he said.

"What kind of bonds?"

"A and AA bonds with 30-year maturities."

"Okay," I said. "Commissions are better in long bonds, but why not put them into bonds with shorter maturities and higher and more liquid grades, such as AAA bonds and government issues?" I told him the story of my Navy days when the plane crashed into the helicopter because the commanders had failed to examine what could go wrong with existing procedures.

Irving assured me he was on top of things, but I was not convinced that he had really given serious thought to what a stock market decline would do to the bond market.

Unfortunately, my fears were realized. The stock market did go into a broad decline, and bids disappeared in the market for lower grade bonds with longer maturities. Irving could not sell his bonds at any price. Bonds with 30-year maturities and $1,000 face values had bids as low as $500 to $600. High-grade bonds fared better because there was more demand for them. The falling prices for the bonds his clients held were worse than the declines in the stock market, and he was locked in. When the stock market decline was over and he wanted to get back in at the bottom, he would face huge bond losses. In effect, he had no recourse but to wait for bond prices to recover or to hold them until maturity. Either way, his days as a big producer were over, and he retired later that year. Chalk up another victim of Murphy's Law.

Over the years, I often wondered who Murphy was. Checking the Internet, I was surprised to learn that the original Murphy's Law states, "If there are two or more ways to do something, and one of those ways can result in a catastrophe, then someone will do it."

Murphy's full name was Edward A. Murphy Jr. He was born in 1917 and was one of the engineers on the rocket-sled experiments conducted by the Air Force in 1949 to test human acceleration tolerances. One experiment involved a set of 16 accelerometers mounted to different parts of the subject's body. There were two ways each sensor could be glued to its mount. Of course, somebody managed to install all 16 the wrong way. At a news conference a few days later, Murphy made the original pronouncement, and within months, Murphy's Law had spread to various technical cultures, finally reaching Webster's dictionary in 1958. The relentless truth inherent in Murphy's Law has become a persistent thorn in the side of humanity.

In October 1970, I was scheduled to move to a large, new, and very expensive brokerage office and as the manager, I was worried that my office might not survive the added expense in the current environment.

I got an early dose of contrary divergent behavior on the very first day in our office. Before I left for work that morning, I had watched a few minutes of a major morning news show featuring Elliot Janeway, a famous economist, being interviewed. When the newscaster asked him for his view of the stock market and the economy, he replied it was very bearish and that the economy and the stock market would soon be entering a free-fall.

I yelled at my television set, as I frequently do, to avoid being brainwashed, "What in the world is this guy saying? My God! The market has been going down since early in the year and is heavily sold out in the background of a very negative news environment!"

I had not learned about Pareto yet, but my contrarian instincts told me that Janeway was wrong. Later that day, I called a sales meeting to kick off our first day in our new office. I told the salesmen that according to the majority of experts, the outlook was gloomy. "If you believe in contrary thinking," I said, "you have to buy stocks now for your clients."

I continued, "Most of our clients are negative and frightened. Janeway was bearish this morning on national television. I think it is smart to be critical of experts, especially when their views are the same as those of the majority of people."

The stock market had opened lower but never looked back again. It rose sharply over the following days and weeks. A broad new bull market had begun and my new office was profitable from day one. Janeway had turned bearish at the exact bottom of the 1970 bear market!

In Chapter 13, I discuss again the five factors to the Magic T and show you the easiest and least expensive ways to determine their current investment inputs.

CHAPTER 9

Increasing Your Knowledge of When to Buy Stocks and When to Stay on the Sidelines

In Chapter 4, I point out there are times to invest when the probabilities are greatly in your favor. There is also a time when you should stay out of the market, regardless of how favorable you think the probabilities might be. If you are under a period of stress, such as a major relocation, divorce, health disability, or even a sudden windfall of money, do not become involved in the stock market.

After graduating from college in 1960, I entered Naval Officer Candidate School (OCS) in Newport, Rhode Island. I was wearing most of my belongings and had stuffed the rest into a couple of cardboard boxes.

The first person I met at OCS was a smartly dressed graduate of UCLA. He even had a suitcase. I was a little embarrassed but quickly exchanged my civilian clothes for the Navy uniform I was issued and threw my old clothes away.

The first semester at OCS was a monumental struggle for me. I had made it through my schooling up to that point with the help of a good memory and a lot of bluffing. Now I was cracking the books with the crème of the crop, graduates of Yale, Notre Dame, and other prestigious schools. I just could not keep up with them.

Candidates like me who were getting failing grades were confined to the base on weekends. For the first two months of the program, I did not step off campus. Not only was I in trouble academically, but also in other areas of officer training. For example, we had to polish our shoes until they reflected the inspecting officer's face like a mirror, and the bedding on our bunk beds had to be tucked in so tight that a quarter would bounce when tossed on the bed. I received demerits for my sloppiness and began to despair that I would never make it as a naval officer.

At the start of my program in Newport, there were 619 candidates in the 50th class at OCS. Only 495 graduated. The rest flunked out to face boot camp training as enlisted men, along with high school dropouts and others without a college education. They would never become officers.

I was sliding downhill from the beginning and my classmates were not much help. Halfway through the first year, we were asked to name one classmate we felt would not make it through the course. I was crushed to see my name on the list. The future looked bleak indeed.

In my despair, I called my mother and poured out to her my disappointment in myself as a failure in the officer-training program.

"Mom," I said, "I'm flunking out, and I'm going to end up as an enlisted man, a common sailor, at Great Lakes."

"George," she asked, "where are you now?"

"I'm at the base. They won't let me off base because my grades are so lousy."

"How's the food? What did you eat today?"

"Good, Mom. I just had some oatmeal, but—"

"Are you sleeping well?"

"Yes, but—"

"That's good, Son! Good!"

At that moment, the burden of all of my worries and concerns about my dismal performance rolled off my back.

"Mom, I've got to run. I'll call you back," I blurted into the phone.

I hung up and started laughing. I laughed until tears rolled down my cheeks. I felt as light as air, as frivolous as a feather. I had been liberated from my fear, knowing that my mother did not care if I was an officer or a sailor. All she cared about was that I was eating and sleeping well and not in trouble. She did not mind that I was confined to base; at least I was not running around in town making mischief.

My experience at Officer Candidate School turned a corner. I became a motivated learner, a rapid assimilator of the facts and skills poured out in lectures and practice sessions. I owe my turn-around to my mother for being the simple, loving person she was. When I had called her, I was in the bottom 10 percent of my class. By the time I graduated, I was in the top 10 percent. In addition, the list of prospective failures composed by my classmates no longer included my name.

Does stress make a difference in a person's performance? Absolutely. Arthur Kane, an investor in Miami, bought stock on margin until he was deep into debt with an $11 million portfolio all purchased with funds borrowed from Merrill Lynch. On Black Monday, October 19, 1987, the Dow Jones Industrial Average dropped 22.6 percent, the largest single-day decline in history.

Kane was so distraught that he walked into Merrill's North Miami office and opened fire with an M-19 pistol. He killed the manager, hit a broker, leaving him paralyzed for life, and then killed himself.

The next day, the market recovered and went on to soar to new heights. Those who held on got all their money back. If only Kane had waited one more day, things would have worked out for him. Instead, at his moment of greatest suffering, he panicked. Shakespeare said, "Take heart, suffering, when it climbs highest, lasts but a little time." It is unfortunate that Kane lost control of his emotions, and at his moment of greatest suffering, panicked. Save major decisions for a time when you are not under stress or otherwise overly emotional.

In Chapters 8, 13, and 14, I discuss the Magic T. The Magic T is a simple technique that I developed over the years to keep my emotions in check, especially when making any major long-term decision, including the amount of risk I am willing to take in the stock market at any given time.

Any investor who uses insider trading analysis as an important tool in deciding what to buy and when to buy it is, by nature, a contrarian. Insiders, in general, are going against the grain of popular opinion. They sell as stocks go up and buy as stocks go down. This is their nature. When the stock market is in the throes of a major decline and fear abounds, the only buyers of stocks will be insiders and other contrarian investors and those who follow insiders. Eighty percent of all money managers will be selling stock at major bottoms to meet redemptions by panicky investors. These forced sales are always accompanied by negative news into an already deeply oversold stock market. As contrarians, we live for times like these. The Magic T will be 100 percent weighted to the buy side, and the signal is usually early (one week to three months). We will have had sufficient time to prepare for the decline and the bad news that accompanies it.

Severe market times are always accompanied by great fear at the bottoms, and the Magic T is instrumental in keeping us calm and centered so that we can buy stocks at the bottom, against a backdrop of negative stock market and economic news.

However, there is another time when our emotions run wild, and being on the sidelines might make us anxious. That time occurs when the market has soared to new highs and the backdrop of good news and positive sentiment is at extremely high levels. As contrarians, we must always be on the opposite side of what the masses are doing. At market tops, all of the news is super. Analysts and professional money managers are bullish, market letter writers are ebullient, and the public is making money and buying on margin. At these times, the Magic T will be flashing a Stay Out signal.

In my opinion, market tops are tougher on emotions than bottoms. Everyone loves a bargain and that includes bargain stocks. If we have not been buried in the decline and have been sitting on the sidelines, waiting for our Magic T signal, it is easy. What is not easy, however, is to be on the sidelines when day after day, others are making money. Even worse, they often remind you about it.

I know how hard it is emotionally to have been out of the stock market while it continued going up. In May 1987, the Magic T turned negative. The market did not break until mid-October and it had its biggest rise from May to September. I recall doubting myself about having become yesterday's news or a dinosaur. As usual, most of these doubts came in the month just before the crash.

Another tough emotional experience took place in late June 2003. After having had three Magic T buy signals in July and October 2002 and then again in March 2003, the Magic T advised to start selling stocks and to Stay Out. It was very painful to see the market rise to new recovery highs in early January, seven months following the sell signal. Without a technique to keep my emotions in check, I would never be able to stay with my contrarian approach to the stock market. I would cave in and buy stocks, and most likely I would be with the masses, holding the bag at the top. After all, I am Romanian and my romance heritage would be my downfall in times of emotional periods.

Fortunately, I have the Magic T to keep me in check. A contrarian basis always reminds me that the key to market success is "Bought well, half sold." Having bought well makes the job of selling a lot easier. When the Magic T flashes its usual early sell signal, I know I will have to take some emotional pain as the market enters the last and usually insane, parabolic phase. I am always comforted by the fact that I made money on the last Magic T buy signal and another one will most assuredly follow. In the meantime, I can work on my golf swing or skiing technique while I wait.

What should you do at times when your emotions are running high? Nothing; put your money into a one-year Treasury bill and wait for your thoughts to become clearer. A few years ago, a friend called and told me he had just received a big windfall. His grandfather had left him $700,000 and he had just received the money. He was a secure person, happy and well adjusted. I told him to buy a one-year T-bill and call me when it matured. He seemed confused and wanted to know why he should wait. I explained that a lump sum of money can actually add to your stress level, because there are many decisions that have to be made, such as disputes among the family, requests of financial help from friends and family, taxes, and the many choices of where to put your money. Today they even have a name for this stress. It is called Lottery Winner Syndrome, named for the many people who have won millions and then have gone on to destroy their own lives.

In my experience, similar to many of life's lessons, the answers will come from within. The men and women who followed my advice, never had to ask me for complete guidance. Over the following year, the answers came to them. It is a bit like the old Chinese proverb "Stand in one place long enough and just about everything will pass in front of you."

CHAPTER 10

How to Find Information on The Vital Few and The Trivial Many

It is time to discuss the best places to find what you need to know about Insiders, Advisory Sentiment, Mood of the Media, Mood of Your Friends and Acquaintances, and the State of the Stock Market. Discussed in Chapter 8, they make up the ingredients of the Magic T.

Insiders: There are many web sites on the Internet that offer insider trading information. However, I have found little value in most of them (Pareto's 80:20 Rule at work again). The site that I recommend is Yahoo.com.

Yahoo! is free. You go to the web site and click on Finance. You then type in a stock symbol and click on Insider. Find the link that indicates Insider Transactions. It will show recent insider trading in your stock of interest. I recommend you ignore everything except open market trading. In my opinion, everything except open market insider activity is noise and should be filtered out. It is very important to know the backgrounds of the insiders in your stocks. Find the link that states Profile. At the lower right of the Profile page, you will see a link that states Full List under View Insiders. You then can review the biographies of those insiders who are trading in your stocks of interest, including how long they have been with the company. It is always of interest when an insider has been with the company for some time and either buys for the first time or dramatically increases his or her purchase dollar value from past transactions. Pay special interest to actions of Officers and Vice-Presidents. These are men and women on the firing line, and money is very dear to them. What could be easier? The Yahoo! insider site is neutral in that it does not offer any stock recommendations. It is my view that you should find your own stocks and then check to see what insiders are doing. Most market letter writers who recommend stocks based on insider analysis have little training and, in my opinion, have just enough knowledge to be dangerous. Remember my thesis that insiders sell into price strength and buy into price weakness. What you want to look for are new purchases where insiders are buying as the stock goes up, as this implies more good news is coming. When insiders are buying a depressed turnaround stock, then you want to see them increasing their ownership percentages by at least 30 percent. Insiders who are just nibbling their depressed company's stock price could be conducting window dressing for investor good will. Another useful web site is vickers-stock.com. Here you can access, free, 24 months of insider history on any stock. Their companion report, the *Weekly Insider Report*, provides insider trades along with the Vickers Insider Sell/Buy Ratio.

An easy way to see if insiders are buying into price strength or selling into price weakness is to go into BigCharts (BigCharts.com). This is a free web site that allows you to see a price pattern for the past 20 years. I usually just check out the past six months to see if insiders are buying on the way up or selling on the way down. I also spend a lot of time on StockCharts.com. This is another free site that provides me with point and figure charts. I like point and figure charts because the signals are clear cut and it is easy to get price objectives. Point and figure charts work well with positive and negative insiders patterns. Actually, StockCharts.com provides price objectives so you do not have to calculate them.

InvestorsIntelligence.com uses the Vickers Sell/Buy Ratio for clues to overall insider attitudes toward the stock market. I recommend you ignore their interpretation of the Sell/Buy Ratio when they forecast the year ahead. The Magic T, which is discussed in Chapter 11, uses current insider attitudes toward the market, not projections of where the stock market will be a year later.

I am concerned about recommending the Vickers Sell/Buy Ratio because I am not sure how they are treating multiple trades by the same insider in any given month. Prior to September 1, 2003, insiders, in general, filed once a month. An insider who traded five times during the month would list one aggregated transaction. Since September 1, 2003, however, all insiders are required to file within two business days of their trades. That same insider who filed only one aggregated trade must now file his or her Form 4 reporting statement five times. At Muzea Insider Consulting Services, we aggregate all insider trades each month so that our current sell/buy ratios compare favorably to our historical records. We know we are comparing apples to apples, but I am not sure that other companies, like Vickers, that keep their own insider buy/sell ratios are not comparing apples to oranges. Another free web site that provides insights as to insider attitudes toward the stock market is lanceranalytics.com, which uses the dollar value of insider sales in its analysis.

My individual subscription service's main goal is to teach subscribers that by using the Magic T to control their emotions, they can know when to be in the stock market and when to be out. A secondary service I provide is to offer my interpretation of insider trading in subscriber stocks of interest. I have observed that some of my newer subscribers have a tendency to automatically assume any insider buying in stocks they like is a positive confirmation. Nothing could be further from the truth. Although insider analysis is an art form subject to many interpretations, there are some common themes that if mastered will help one become very proficient at interpreting insider actions. Some of these tips have been covered before, but in this case a little repetition will not hurt. The following six insights are the most important to consider:

1. Insiders normally buy into price weakness and sell into price strength; therefore it is important to look for deviations from this behavior.
2. Stocks that have insider selling (three or more insiders) into price weakness should be considered seriously as candidates to sell.
3. Insider trading by operating officers is more predictive than those of other insiders, especially outside directors.
4. When analyzing insider trading, it is important to observe previous trading patterns to see if the current trade is in line with or a divergence from normal behavior.

5. When insiders buy stocks that are depressed in price and out of favor, much of the time the buying is a sign of value, but sometimes it is simply designed to ignite investor confidence. The best way to determine which is which is to review carefully the dollar value of the purchases. If the insiders had sold previously at higher levels, they should be buying back at least 25 percent of what they sold; otherwise, they could be window dressing.

6. Most of the time one should look for clusters of insider buyers who have all made decisions to buy stock in their companies. However, sometimes a single trade can be predictive, especially when the buying insider has a good trading history in that stock or the purchase is an unusual divergence from past behavior.

These tips will go a long way to getting you started on the interesting and profitable journey that monitoring insider behavior provides. Over the years, I have developed favorite insider patterns that I look for. Analyzing insider behavior is not brain surgery. But like brain surgery, the more you do it, the better you get at it. Insider patterns occur over and over again and it will be just a matter of time before you get really good at it and ultimately find your own favorites. The field of insider trading also holds may untested hypotheses. The sooner you get started at analyzing insider behavior in stocks of your interest, the better.

Advisory Sentiment: Regular watchers of financial television programs such as CNBC will get this information free on the air, usually on Wednesday mornings. The weekly magazine *Barron's* has a Market Laboratory section that provides a number of sentiment indicators, including the American Association of

Individual Investors, which I have found to be a great reverse indicator at extreme points.

Mood of the Media: This one you have to do on your own, but it is easy. I do it by simply watching CNBC and CNN as often as I can and especially after a market decline or surge. I want to see who is being paraded out to see if their mood is the same as the Advisory Sentiment Indicator. If insider behavior is opposite, look for a turn.

In July 2002, I turned short-term bullish based on my analysis of The Vital Few versus The Trivial Many. I thought we would have a good trading rally until early September when I thought the rally would then end because of institutional tax loss selling that usually begins in early September and ends on October 31, but I needed a trigger to get me to act on my short-term bullishness. I observed CNBC's Maria Bartiromo advising viewers to learn how to sell short. I then had everything I needed to make a low-risk trade, buying the exchange-traded fund SPY, which mirrors the action of the S&P 500. I sold the SPY's at an 11 percent profit the first week of September. The Vital Few versus The Trivial Many worked like a charm.

Mood of Friends and Acquaintances: Again, you are on your own, but this, too, is very easy. Just identify who among your friends is very emotional, especially when it comes to money. I have maintained contacts with a few stockbrokers whom I have known for years. I usually call them at important turning points to ask them the mood of their customers. It is amazing how frightened they are at the bottom and ebullient they can be at the top. When I was a stockbroker with E.F. Hutton in New York, I had a client that was always wrong at decision time. I used to call him and tell him about a stock I liked. If he liked the idea, I never offered it to my clients, including him. If he did not like the idea, I aggressively marketed the stock. Even the other brokers would ask me to call my reverse indicator to see if he liked their ideas.

My client was a very nice man, but his wife had left him, he had trouble with his kids, and he always complained about his job. When he finally closed his account after he had lost his job, the other brokers and I had a party in his honor. We were depressed for him and us.

Pay attention (again stay aware and be observant) to what people are saying about the stock market at cocktail parties, in stores, wherever people gather and talk. It could be very helpful. This is old advice, but when the person who shines your shoes tells you he is making money in the stock market, or starts to ask you questions about the stock market, watch out.

When you find a good reverse indicator, nurture that person and stay in contact. He or she will come in handy at turning points.

In March 2000, the height of the technology bubble, I noticed that insiders were selling huge dollar amounts of these stocks. Like everyone else, I thought the new economy was truly a once in a lifetime event, though the insider selling in the stocks that I owned troubled me. Two experiences caused me to sell out in April. I live in a private golf course community in southwest Reno. Wednesday was Ladies Day so I went over to play at a local municipal golf course. I was teamed up with a young man who was walking while I drove a cart.

While we were waiting at the second tee, he asked me what I did for a living. When I told him that I monitored insider trading for institutions, he seemed very interested and went on tell me that he was a day trader and had quit his job as an accountant for Grant Thornton. I asked him how he was doing. He told me he was making $3,000 a week buying options on technology stocks. He said his grandmother had died and had left him $200,000. I told him he was making an unsustainable return and advised him to be careful and reminded him of a few stock market bubbles such as: the conglomerate boom and bust in the late 1960s, the boom and bust of real estate investment trusts in the early 1970s, and the oil and gas stock crash in the early 1980s. He looked at me like I was a dinosaur and did not comment. For the rest of the afternoon, I just focused on golf.

A month later, my wife and I were enjoying a four-day stay at the Green Valley Spa in St. George, Utah. We love this spa because they know how to pamper you, and we enjoy hiking the surrounding mountains with other spa guests. There were three walks every day of varying length and difficulty. Maria went on the most grueling, and I went on the easiest one. I love to talk and the slow pace was just fine with me.

On the second day, I was walking near the back with a woman named Sarah and her daughter Kim, who was probably in her early thirties. During the walk, they asked what I did. I replied that I monitored insider trading for institutions. Kim seemed especially interested. She told me she had left her full-time career as an electrical engineer and was trading the stock market for a living. She added that her mother helped her with the analysis.

I asked Kim about her experience with the market and she told me that she and her mother had started investing in 1998 and had done quite well. I asked her where she got information on the stock market and individual stocks. They both talked about how great CNBC was for new ideas and were avid readers of *For-*

tune magazine and *Barron's*. They also had obtained many good ideas from the Internet, especially The Street.Com.

I told Kim and Sarah that I had been a guest on *The Nightly Business Report* and *CNBC* many times as well as having had interviews in *Fortune, Barron's*, and TheStreet.Com. I wanted them to know that I was a seasoned professional, and then advised them to be careful because I had a sense that the market seemed very similar to the early 1980s when oil was $40 a barrel and analysts saw no negatives to further price rises. I shared the story about the dentists in Florida who were selling or closing their practices to move to Houston to drill for oil and gas as well.

Again, I got the "what a dinosaur!" look, so I sighed lightly, changed the subject, and moved ahead to talk to another person. Later that evening, I told Maria that I thought we were facing a technology bubble and told her about my talk with Sarah and Kim. That prompted Maria to ask me if she should sell out, following my advice the next day.

When I returned to my office in Reno, I held a meeting with my staff. We had two administrative assistants, three insider analysts, my secretary, and a programmer. I told them about the fellow I had played golf with a month earlier and advised them to be very careful and to build cash reserves, adding that in the 1980s, some of the brokers in my office in Florida had been making $25,000 a month focusing on oil and gas stocks for their clients. After the oil bubble broke, some of them were seen driving cabs around South Florida. The staff was amused and Michael, my senior analyst, pointed out that we would never know what happened to my golfing partner and most other investors who left good jobs to trade the stock market for a living.

Eighteen months later in September 2001, I visited some clients in New York. The market had been in a long decline, and the technology bubble had popped with most of these stocks in well-defined downtrends. After a couple of days of conferences, I took the red-eye back to Reno. When I got out of the baggage area at 3:00 in the morning, I walked to an area designated for taxis. One pulled up and I got into the back. The driver seemed young and intelligent, but I was exhausted and closed my eyes for a quick nap during the 20-minute drive to my home. Trying to make small talk, he looked at me through his rear view mirror and asked what I did. As usual, I said, "I monitor insider trading for institutions." The young man replied, "I thought it was you. Don't you remember me? We played a round of golf about a year and a half ago."

I looked at him incredulously and asked him what had happened. For the rest of the trip, he went on to explain how he had been killed in the market trading tech stocks. He told me he had only $20,000 left and had developed a stomach ulcer to add to his misery. He was driving a cab to regain his health and would never buy another stock again, he said. He was looking forward to getting back to being an accountant.

The next day I told Maria and my staff about the taxi driver. It was incredible that my prediction for this young man had come true and that it took such a short period for it to happen. I never found out what happened to Sarah and her daughter Kim. I can only hope that their ultimate fate was better than my one-day golfing friend's.

I am sure you get the point. It is very important to listen to your friends and people you meet at random. When you see a trend developing and acknowledge that you think the same, you should start to look hard at your own position. Most likely, you are part of The Trivial Many. It is okay to be part of the masses sometimes, but not okay to do it unknowingly. Once you recognize you are hooked, you then can check the other indicators to see if the pieces fit. If insiders are negative and investment advisors and the public are bullish, follow The Vital Few; sell your stocks and be prepared to sit patiently on the sidelines until the odds of success are once again in your favor.

State of the Stock Market: This is the final piece you need to know. The easiest and least expensive way to determine the state of the market is to go into BigCharts.com and look at a five-year history of the Dow Jones Industrial Average. A picture is worth a thousand words. You can easily see if the Dow is in an uptrend or downtrend by studying the chart and comparing its current price to the overall trend of its average price for 200 days. Any stockbroker, full service or discount, can easily tell you what the Dow's 200-day moving average is. If the 200-day average is rising and the current price is above the 200-day line, the market is in an uptrend. If the current price is below the 200-day line and the line is heading down, then the overall market is in a downtrend.

A simple way to see if the stock market is oversold or overbought is to check the Dow's current price relative to its average over the past 200 days. If the current price is 10 percent to 20 percent in either direction of its 200-day moving average, it is either overbought or oversold, depending on the direction of current prices. Most technical analysts consider the market to be deeply oversold or overbought when the current price is more than 20 percent away from its current reading.

A technical indicator that I have used for years to help me know when the broad stock market is oversold or overbought is the

Commodity Channel Indicator (CCI). Although the CCI was originally designed for commodities, I have found it works very well with stocks and major indexes. The CCI usually oscillates between +200 and −200. Daily readings outside these ranges imply moderately overbought/oversold conditions. Weekly readings outside these ranges imply deeply overbought/oversold conditions.

I created my Magic T subscription service for the individual investor based on suggestions from readers who figured they could save time and money by reading my weekly analysis of the five Magic T ingredients discussed earlier. You can check out my subscription service on magict.info, and I am happy to send back copies for your review.

CHAPTER 11

Technical Analysis and Insider Trading

THE FIRST EDITION OF THIS BOOK WAS A SMALL SELF-PUBLISHED BOOK, and while I was pleased that many readers loved the concise and succinct way it was written, I believed I could expand it by adding more chapters on investing, including styles of investing and technical analysis.

As I began to write these additional pages, I canvassed the subscribers of my retail service, the Weekly Magic T (MagicT.info). I was surprised and pleased by their enthusiastic response. Still, I was concerned. I wanted to keep the book in an autobiographical format, making it easy for first time investors to understand that knowing when to be in the market and when to be out was the most important part of their development into being a successful investor. Easy reading makes it that much easier. The second concern I had was writing a chapter on technical analysis. I know that technical analysis is very useful and almost hand in glove with insider trading analysis. I use point and figure charts to help me time buying and selling of individual stocks. One of the ingredients of the Magic T, State of the Stock Market, in fact, is a technical process.

I had no problem writing the new pages in my expanded version of *The Vital Few vs. The Trivial Many*. I knew technical analysis would be a challenge for me, however. I use technical analysis and understand its importance. However, I reasoned that if I could find an experienced technician to blend my insider buy and sell signals into the technical picture, the overall value of my book would be enhanced.

I believe my subscribers can and should use technical analysis to tweak my Magic T market calls, which are early on both the buy and sell side. The key is to never go against the Magic T, but to work with it. For example, if the Magic T is neutral or has just turned negative and you still want to trade, then use technical analysis on stocks that have insider buying and are in up trends. If you want to short an index or a stock, it would be foolish not to use a technical analysis technique to assist you. The Magic T will tell you how much market risk there is, but a chart analysis will be useful with timing.

I asked a good friend of mine, Matthew Claassen, to write a piece about technical analysis. Mr. Claassen has earned the prestigious Chartered Market Technician (CMT) designation signifying his expertise as a technical analyst and market strategist. Offered by the Market Technicians Association, the CMT designation has been awarded to fewer than 900 professionals over the past 20 years. He can be reached at matthewcmt@thetechnicalview.net. I am pleased to include Matthew Claassen's article.

Technical Analysis and Insider Trading

Definitions and Differences

While many investors have heard the terms fundamental analysis and technical analysis, few understand the significant differences between the two disciplines.

The fundamental analyst uses microeconomic data from a company and its industry to forecast future prices. The fundamental analyst's tools include such things as past earnings, cash flow, and sales trends. Among the underlying beliefs of fundamental analysis is the conviction that all price movement in the market is random and that equity prices seek a fair value as defined by their fundamental qualities.

Technical analysis ignores fundamental data, focusing instead on the information provided in the price and volume of the security itself. Technical analysis can be defined as the study of a security's price and volume for the purpose of identifying or forecasting price trends. The technical analyst works with the belief that not all price movement is random. Prices tend to move in trends and since human behavior tends to repeat itself, these trends tend to repeat.

The use of technical analysis to forecast prices pre-dates fundamental analysis by more than 300 years. Long before any company was required to provide an annual report, technicians were charting stocks and commodity prices and predicting future prices based on chart patterns. In the nearly 400 years since the first chart was used to predict future price movement, the foundation of technical analysis has never changed because that foundation is rooted in human behavior, the behavior of the masses.

Identifying a Trend

Since it is a defining tenet of technical analysis that stocks trend, identifying the trend is the market technician's first duty when analyzing a prospective investment. As the simplest of systems, an investor can be in an investment while it is rising and out of an investment while it is falling by simply correctly identifying the trend.

Because no stock goes straight up or straight down, an up trend is defined as a series of higher highs and higher lows. A downtrend is defined as a series of lower highs and lower lows.

Figure 11.1 shows an idealized drawing of a trending stock. The highs marked 1, 3, and 5 are the higher highs of a rising trend and are followed by higher lows marked 2 and 4. As the trend changes from up to down, the lower highs indicated by points B and D are each followed by lower lows C and E.

To aid in identifying a trend or a change in a trend, we use moving averages and trendlines. To draw a trendline identifying

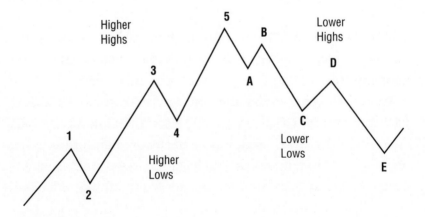

FIGURE 11.1   Defining a Trend

rising trends, simply connect the higher lows and extend the line into the future. By connecting the price lows of a rising trend, we can easily identify a change in trend as the point in time when the price of the stock declines below the trendline. The trendline for a declining trend is drawn by connecting the highs of a falling stock. That point where the trendline is violated is the point where the declining trend is over.

Stocks do not always go up or down. Sometimes they travel sideways, staying within a defined price range for a long period of time. These sideways movements are usually just a period of rest before a stock continues along the prevailing trend. Because of this, it is often wise to use the violation of a trendline as a warning of a change in trend. Confirmation of the end of a rising trend can be realized when the stock price falls below the previous low, creating a lower low. Confirmation of the end of a declining trend can be realized when the price of the stock rises above the previous high, creating a higher high.

In Figure 11.2, I have illustrated a rising and declining trend for General Electric (GE) from 1995 to April 2004. To grasp the power of this simple tool, imagine you had purchased GE in 1995 and held on to your shares until they broke the trendline and formed a lower low in 2001. Look at the bear market you would have avoided.

We can also use moving averages to identify trends. In Figure 11.3, I have inserted a 40-week (200-day) moving average as a dashed line. A moving average is calculated by adding the closing prices and dividing the sum by the time period used. So a 40-week moving average would sum the weekly closing prices for the previous 40 weeks and divide the total by 40. A 200-day moving average would add the closing prices for the last 200 days and

FIGURE 11.2   General Electric and Trendlines

divide by 200. Since a market week is made up of five days, a 200-day and 40-week moving average are virtually identical.

The same rules are used with a moving average as we used with the trendline, requiring a break in the moving average accompanied by the price falling below the previous low or rising above the previous high to identify a change in trend. As you can see from Figure 11.3, the results would be the same as with the trendlines. Many investors prefer the use of a moving average to trendlines because a moving average can be easily plotted using many of the free charting programs found on the Internet.

Tools

There are many dozens of tools available to the market technician and many different schools of thought practiced under

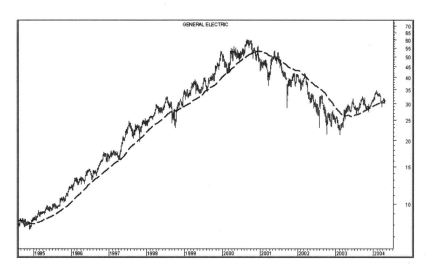

FIGURE 11.3   General Electric and 40-Week Moving Average

the definition of technical analysis. This includes the use of different types of charts like point and figure, candlesticks, and bar charts as well as different theories on market behavior such as cycles and Elliott Wave analysis. Most go well beyond the scope of what I wish to accomplish here. For this chapter, I have chosen a few specific tools for their ease of use as well as their effectiveness.

When analyzing any investment, I prefer to divide my analysis into three categories: tools that are leading indicators, coincident indicators, and lagging indicators. Leading indicators help warn us of a potential change in trend. A coincident indicator tells us when the trend has changed, and a lagging indicator confirms that the investment is firmly on a new trend. This effective methodology is no different from what we would expect of an economist or fundamental analyst. The analytical thought process is very much the same.

Leading Indicators

One of the most reliable leading indicators in technical analysis is volume. If we break down the rise and fall of any stock price into the simple components of demand and supply, volume is one of its best measures. The volume of any stock is simply the number of shares traded in a particular amount of time. It may be a day, week, month, or even intraday periods. For an index, volume is the sum of the shares traded in all of its components.

To best understand the value in using volume, we have to first understand that the deciding factor for whether a stock rises or falls today, tomorrow, or next week is simply the ratio of supply and demand. If more shares are being purchased (demand) than sold (supply), the stock will rise in price. If more shares are being sold than purchased, it will fall in price. However, because supply and demand is a ratio, a stock can rise if demand (buying) stays the same but supply (selling) falls. The converse is also true. If the amount of shares being sold remains the same but the amount of shares being purchased declines, the stock can fall.

This concept is important because in order for a stock to have a sustainable uptrend, it must have increasing demand. As a matter of fact, there is an old Wall Street saying I use when I teach basic analysis: "A stock can fall of its own weight, but it takes volume to rise." In other words, when a stock can begin a major decline without increased volume, it falls of its own weight. But for a sustainable uptrend we must see an increase in volume, an increase in demand.

As a rule of thumb, a stock that is rising on higher volume is rising on increased demand, a healthy sign. A stock that is falling on increased volume is falling on increased supply, an unhealthy sign. A stock that is rising on lower volume is probably rising due to lower selling pressure instead of increased buying. This usually leads to lower prices. When a stock is falling on lower volume, we must use other tools to determine the nature of the decline.

A classic illustration of volume can be found in Figure 11.4, a weekly chart of Amazon.com (AMZN) from 1997 to mid-2004. Clearly the advance during 1997–1998 is on dramatically increased volume, pure rising demand. The peak in volume in late 1998 preceded the peak price in the stock by nearly a year, a strong leading indication that demand was drying up. Thus Amazon.com continued higher from late 1998 to mid-1999 on lower volume and then revisited the mid-1999 high later that year on still lower volume, all a sign that buying enthusiasm was falling but selling had not yet increased. Because AMZN had risen so strongly and consistently for several years,

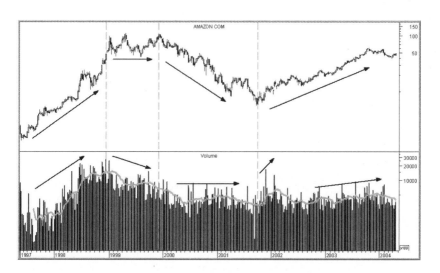

FIGURE 11.4   Amazon.com and Weekly Volume

investors' expectations were for a continued rise in price. Thus few were willing to let go of their holdings. At the same time, Amazon.com had risen far enough that many investors were not able to justify new purchases in the stock. The stock was no longer rising due to increased demand. It was rising because so few investors wanted to sell.

After the final peak in late 1999, Amazon.com began what was to become a severe bear market. It did so with declining volume in early 2000. If an investor was looking for rising volume during the decline to confirm that AMZN was in trouble, they would have missed their opportunity to exit at a high price.

Amazon.com bottomed in late 2001 and began to rise on significantly higher volume; demand was increasing again. The astute market technician would have recognized that the landscape had changed and the trend was likely to change as well. Higher volume continued for about four months, long enough to pull AMZN up from near $5 per share to nearly $15 per share. Volume then returned to more normal levels with a mild bullish rise, reflecting increased demand.

In addition to volume itself, there is an indicator based on volume that I find to be an invaluable tool. This indicator, developed by Joe Granville, is called On Balance Volume (OBV).* On Balance Volume is a popular indicator available in virtually every technical analysis software package and every technical analysis web site I know of. The calculation for OBV is simple. It assumes that all the volume for any day that closed up was positive volume. All the volume for any day that closed down was a

---

*Achellis, Steven B. *Technical Analysis from A to Z*. McGraw-Hill, 1995, pp. 207–209.

negative. We then add the positive and negative volumes to reveal the indicator.

When the On Balance Volume line is rising, it means that the volume on the up days is higher than the volume on the down days, a sign the stock is being accumulated. When the OBV line is falling, it means that volume on the down days is higher than volume on up days, a sign the stock is under distribution. Often, we will see the On Balance Volume rise to new highs or fall to new lows ahead of the stock, making it a very useful leading indicator.

A good example of the use of On Balance Volume can be seen in Figure 11.5, a weekly chart of Nextel Communications (NXTL). For the seven months from October 2002 through May 2003, Nextel was caught in a sideways consolidation. The stock

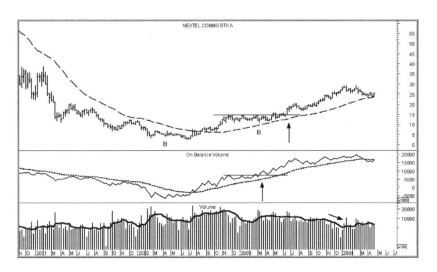

FIGURE 11.5   Nextel Communications and Volume Indicators
(B = insider buy signals)
Source: Published by Muzea Insider Consulting Services, LLC

was not strong enough to move higher or weak enough to fall. For a while, the OBV was also range bound. Then in March 2003, the OBV indicator broke to a new high ahead of the stock. Even though Nextel could not move higher, the volume indicator was telling us that there was more volume on the up days than on the down days and that the stock was under accumulation. Three months later, NXTL broke out from its consolidation pattern and doubled in price within six months. As an aside, it is also worth noting that volume began to decline in October 2003, nearly three months ahead of the most recent high.

Insider buy signals can add value to technical indicators such as On Balance Volume. For example, in Figure 11.5, we see two instances where insider transactions resulted in buy signals. The first was in April 2002, when at that time Nextel was still declining and still in a bear trend. Volume was contracting but the On Balance Volume was just beginning to create a positive divergence with price. A positive divergence is when the indicator rises, making higher lows or higher highs, while the price is still declining. The insider transaction buy signal was a great leading indication of the coming change in trend. Volume began to increase in July; then, in August, the stock broke above its 200-day moving average signaling the downtrend was complete.

The second insider buy signal was in March 2003. This was at the same time the On Balance Volume also provided a leading indication of Nextel's coming advance. In both cases, adding the insider buy signal to our list of leading indicators strengthened our confidence in the analysis and our conviction to take action.

Another good example of On Balance Volume is seen in Figure 11.6. In the early part of 2000, Micron Technology (MU) had advanced sharply from $30 per share to nearly $100. In spite of

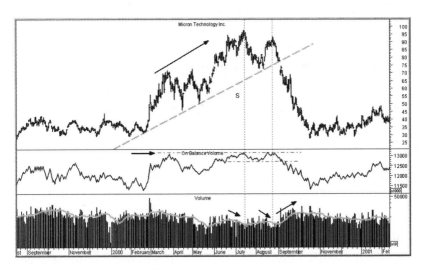

FIGURE 11.6   Micron Technology and Volume Indicators
(S = insider sell signal)
Source: Published by Muzea Insider Consulting Services, LLC

such a strong advance, the OBV was unable to make a higher high. The On Balance Volume was no stronger at Micron's peak price in July of 2000 than it had been at the lower peak in March of that year. We call this a negative divergence, when the price of the investment makes a higher high but the indicator does not. This negative divergence was a leading indicator warning.

In addition to the warning from On Balance Volume we can see that volume itself contracted as MU made its high in July and then contracted again as the stock made a second high in August. All of these signs together are a clear warning that Micron was losing its strength and might soon lose its up trend. Sure enough, MU broke below its trendline below a previous low in September of 2000 on increasing volume.

For Micron Technology, the insider transaction sell signal

came as the stock was making new all time highs. This is a point; most investors would never consider selling because their fear of missing out on the upside is greater than their fear of loss. But when we add the insider sell signal to the signals we saw in our volume indicators, we see strong reasons to step aside or take a more cautious stance.

Although the On Balance Volume has a strong tendency to lead the price of a stock, there are times when this indicator does not lead or leads by very little. In Figure 11.7 of Micron Technology, we can see an example of a very short lead time between On Balance Volume and the stock price.

In early 2003, Micron Technology was still in a severe downtrend. The stock had collapsed from nearly $100 per share only a few years earlier to just above $5 per share. In mid-March of

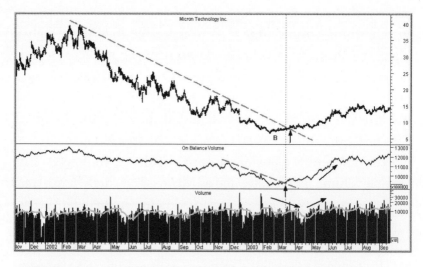

FIGURE 11.7   Micron Technology and Volume Indicators
(B = insider buy signal)
Source: Published by Muzea Insider Consulting Services, LLC

2003, the On Balance Volume indicator broke above its declining trendline showing potential accumulation even though volume was contracting.

When insider buying precedes a break above a downtrend, the chances of a whipsaw or false break put is dramatically reduced. The price of Micron's stock broke above the downtrend line that had served as resistance. With volume still declining, the stock was unable to build on the positive trendline break until May, when volume began to increase notably and the OBV indicator began to rise steeply. Then in early June, the price followed the indicators higher. Insider buying prior to a technical breakout clearly adds validity and increases the chances of success.

Figure 11.8 is our final example of volume indicators. Here we

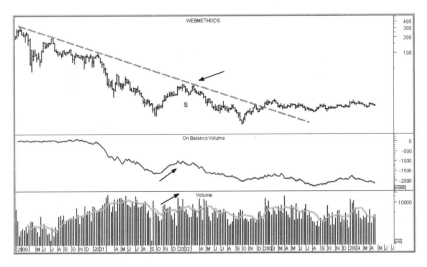

FIGURE 11.8 Webmethods and Volume Indicators

(S = insider sell signal)

Source: Published by Muzea Insider Consulting Services, LLC

see Webmethods (WEBM) from the beginning of 2000 to 2004. From 2000 through 2002, Webmethods was in a severe down trend having fallen from a high of $336 per share to a low under $5 in late 2002. For our example, I want to focus on the low in September 2001 and the bounce that followed.

In late 2001, WEBM had been declining rapidly for nearly two years and sentiment was very bearish. Much of the decline was on heavy volume, but volume contracted going into September 2001. Then off that September low, we saw the stock rise on increased volume and the On Balance Volume indicator expanded. Both are bullish signs.

I would admit the bounce off the September 2001 low could have been a good short-term trade, but would it have been good for the long-term investor? Obviously, we can see from the chart that Webmethods never broke above its declining trendline and by the end of 2003, it was at an even lower price. The bounce may have been good for a short-term trader, but for the investor it was another opportunity to sell their shares.

I had mentioned that the Webmethods' bounce off the September 2001 low was considered another opportunity for the investor to sell their shares. Well, that is exactly what the insiders were doing.

So, back to the two points I want to make. The first point is that adding knowledge of insider transactions to your toolbox of investment indicators can strengthen your ability to correctly analyze the risk and opportunities in every investment. The second point is that leading indicators warn only of a potential change in trend. We still need to confirm a trend change with our coincident indicator.

Coincident Indicator

The market technician uses a coincident indicator to confirm the warnings provided by the leading indicators and to tell us exactly when a trend has reversed. A coincident indicator is important because a signal from some leading indicators can be reversed before the trend changes and because a leading indicator's signal may be many months ahead of any change in trend.

Of course, the best coincident indicator is the price of the security itself. When the price closes above or below our trendlines, we know the trend has changed. When the price makes a higher high or a lower low, we know the trend has reversed. This may sound trite, but I find it amazing how often investors act too soon based on indicator signals alone, ignoring the price action of the underlying investment, and lose money as a result.

Earlier I stated that it is a defining tenet of technical analysis that stocks trend. Coupled with that belief is a second tenet: The trend remains until proved otherwise. In other words, a market technician will assume the underlying trend continues until the price of the security proves that the trend changed. The reason for this is simple. The key to investing profitably is to have a systematic approach that provides a high probability of success with minimal risk. Where many investors go wrong is they attempt the high profit trade instead of the high probability trade. They attempt to buy at the very bottom of a decline or sell at the very top of an advance. Not only is this a near impossible task but also by attempting it, investors put themselves in a position where the probability of making a mistake, and the probability of loss, is high.

By waiting for the price of the underlying security to reach above or below a trendline or moving average and to make a higher high or a lower low, the investor gives up some of the potential profit that could have been realized had they successfully sold at the day of the absolute top or purchased at the absolute low. In return, however, the investor receives a higher probability that the investment made will result in a profit.

When to buy or when to sell is not always a black or white decision. The reason I stress the three-tiered system of leading, coincident, and lagging indicators is that it offers the investor an entry and exit process. If we first identify the size of each investment, we can then divide that investment into three sections. The first section would be invested or sold with the leading indicator signal, the second section with the coincident indicator, and the final section when the lagging indicator confirms. The leading indicators' signal offers the highest potential reward at the highest level of risk. Risk is reduced once the coincident indicator confirms a trend change, but some of the opportunity is also reduced. Finally, once a lagging indicator has made a final confirmation, the trend or reversal of trend is firmly entrenched and unlikely to reverse soon. The risk to the intermediate term investor is reduced another level, but more potential profit is left on the table.

Where some investors' lower tolerance for risk may dictate which signal they use to enter or exit an investment, many will find that their desire for profit and fear of loss are well balanced when they use each level as a partial entry or exit decision. The process of averaging in an investment as it strengthens or averaging out of an investment as it weakens is a method of managing risk. When you manage risk, profits will follow.

Lagging Indicator

We have talked about the use of moving averages to identify the trend of a security. Moving averages will, by nature, lag the investment price but will also follow that price. Thus we can combine two moving averages to create a simple lagging indicator.

Rather than using the price crossing the moving average as our buy or sell signal, we can use two moving averages and wait until the second (shorter) moving average crosses the first longer) moving average. We call this a "dual moving average crossover system."

Since a picture is worth a thousand words, I have illustrated one such moving average crossover system in Figure 11.9. Here

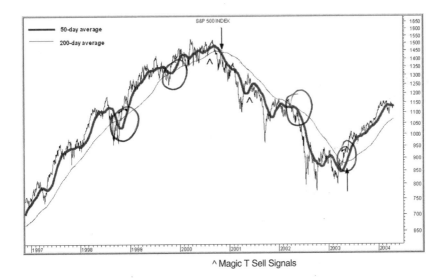

FIGURE 11.9   S&P 500 and Dual Moving Average
Crossover System

we have the S&P 500 from 1997 to April 2004. The thick line is a 50-day moving average. The thin smooth line is the 200-day average. You might notice that even as the S&P 500 was generally rising prior to March 2000, the index broke below the 200-day average on several occasions for a brief period of time. If we used only the price moving above or below the 200-day average as a signal to enter and exit, there would have been many times where we would have exited the index only to reenter at a less advantageous price shortly thereafter. We call this fruitless action a "whipsaw."

Having an entry signal generated only when the 50-day average crosses from below to above the 200-day average and an exit signal generated only when the 50-day average crosses from above to below the 200-day average, we now have a profitable system with fewer whipsaws.

Typically the moving average crossover system using the 50-day and 200-day averages will have very few buy or sell signals. In a trending market, these signals can last for several years and generally occur well after a market high or market low. They also tend to be a reliable indication of the larger trend. In Figure 11.9, only in 1998 was there an occasion where the signal was reversed at a less advantageous price.

This is our lagging indicator. The moving average crossover of a 50-day and 200-day moving average will typically occur after the trendline has been broken and the price itself has crossed the 200-day average. It is important to note that George Muzea's Magic T sell signal in June 2000 came months before the crossover of the 50-day moving average and below the 200-day average in late 2000. When the Magic T signal precedes the technicals, the odds of success are dramatically increased. When the second Magic T sell signal occurred in early 2001, the market's decline was already well established.

Putting It Together

Now take a look at how these three technical analysis tools would have worked together for one of the stocks used earlier.

Nextel Communications is a good example because, as in the real world, the signals from our tools are less than perfect. In Figure 11.10 we can see that in late 1999 and early 2000 volume was declining while the price was still rising. As discussed earlier, this is a clear leading indication of waning demand. Although the signal from total volume was clear, our On Balance Volume indicator did not provide us with any warning.

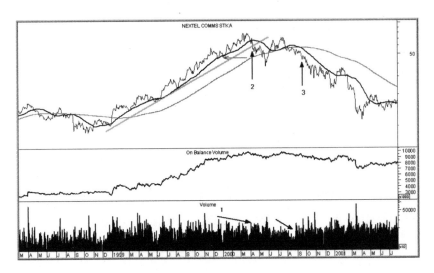

FIGURE 11.10   Nextel Communications and Indicator Signals

In April 2000, Nextel broke below its rising trendline and by the end of May had broken below both the previous low and the 200-day average. The coincident indicator signal was triggered.

Nextel recovered from the May sell-off but on notably lower volume. The fact that volume declined during the recovery is enough to keep any seasoned market technician on the sidelines. Finally in October of 2000, the 50-day average crossed below the 200-day average providing us with the lagging indicator signal.

From the time we noted the first advance on declining volume to the final crossing of the moving averages was nearly one full year. In that time, these technical analysis signals provided a clear indication that NXTL was in a topping process giving adequate time for any investor to exit their position.

Figure 11.11 shows Nextel Communications from January 2000 to the end of 2003. Nextel remained below its trendline and we saw no true strength in the indicators until March 2003, when

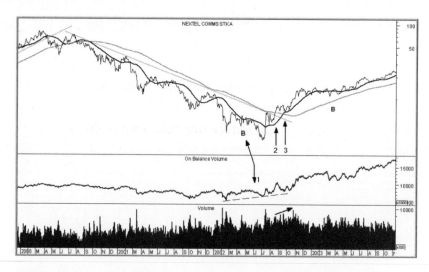

FIGURE 11.11   Nextel Communications and Trend Changes

we received a buy signal from insider activity. That buy signal was quickly followed by a positive divergence in the On Balance Volume in July. Both were strong leading indicators that the downtrend was coming to an end.

Nextel broke above its trendline in late August immediately followed by a break above the 200-day average all on heavy volume. Our coincident indicators had signaled that the downtrend was complete. Finally in October, the 50-day average crossed back above the 200-day average providing a final lagging confirmation of the trend change, and as the stock broke above the previous high, another buy signal was triggered from insider activity.

The bottoming process for Nextel did not take as much time as the topping process. From our first leading indicator signal to the final crossing of our dual moving averages was about six months. This, too, offered plenty of time for an investor to build a position in NXTL and enjoy the bull advance that followed. (See Figure 11.12.)

The methods we have discussed barely scratch the surface of all that technical analysis offers. There is no perfect form of analysis, nothing that will work in all circumstances and all occasions. However, by combining our tools with other forms of analysis such as monitoring insider activity, we can increase our probability of success and reduce our risk. That is the key ingredient to successful investing.

Relative Strength

No discussion of technical analysis is complete without at least a mention of relative strength analysis. Relative strength analysis is

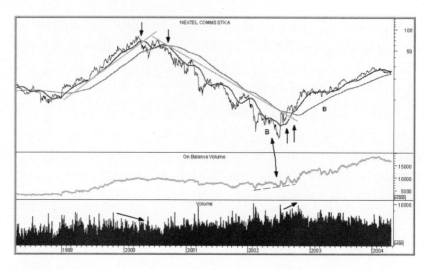

FIGURE 11.12   Nextel Communications and from Bull to Bear and Back Again

among the most proven methods of identifying stocks with the best potential for higher future returns.

Relative strength analysis can be divided into two general categories: Comparative Relative Strength and External Relative Strength.

Comparative Relative Strength is comparing the performance of one investment to another. Typically we see this form of analysis as the performance of an investment compared to an index like the S&P 500. If we use the S&P 500 Index as a proxy for the market, comparing the performance of an investment, sector, or an industry to the Index will help us identify what areas of the market are outperforming the market itself. Another useful method is to apply this relative strength analysis to a stock and its industry. Doing so, we can discover if a stock is outperforming its industry peers.

External Relative Strength is different in that it is a method of comparing the performance of all securities versus each other. The securities are ranked, with the top performing security receiving a rank of 99 or 100 and the lowest performing security receiving a rank of zero or one. External Relative Strength is a more efficient form of relative strength because it quickly identifies the strongest and weakest securities. With Comparative Relative Strength, we know which securities are outperforming an index or industry. With External Relative Strength, we can also quickly identify the strongest or weakest stock in any group or of all securities in our universe of choices.

The best time to buy stocks with the highest external relative strength rankings is when the overall stock market is deeply oversold. Stocks that have held up the best during sharp market drops usually pop first since savvy investors have used the decline to accumulate them. If insiders are among the buyers of these highly ranked stocks during the overall stock market decline, the possibility of exceptional profits in the next up move is greatly enhanced.

CHAPTER 12

Risks and Rewards of Being a Contrarian Investor

IN THE NEXT CHAPTER, I PROVIDE YOU WITH THE COMPLETE STRATEGY for becoming a consistent stock market winner. You already have a good idea about the benefits and some of the hardships of going against the grain. Now, however, is a good time to discuss in more detail the rewards and the difficulties of following a contrarian strategy like mine.

What makes a contrarian? Were we born this way or did life's travails make us into the skeptics we have become. Some people think we were hatched!

I own a few race horses and when they race, usually in the Northeast, I go to the race book at Harrah's in downtown Reno to watch them. In early May 2004, I had a horse that was racing in a $74,000 stakes race and was quite nervous before the race. I was sitting next to an older man who liked another horse in the same race my horse was in. I did not tell him about my horse because I did not want to get into any great dialogue with him.

My horse came in fourth but I was not disappointed because I knew he had been in a tough race and his effort had been good. I did note, however, that my neighbor's horse won and paid $18. I congratulated him on his good handicapping. He turned to me and said, "I didn't bet him!" "Why?" I asked. "Well, there was a young man in line directly ahead of me. I overheard his bet on the horse I liked. He looked like a loser to me so I bet on a different horse."

Astonished that this bettor had taken contrarianism to an extreme, I left the casino without saying another word. On the way home, I wondered how many people are like him in the investing world, simply taking a contrarian stance on just about every one of life's many adventures.

There are many books and articles written about the contrarian style of investing. In my opinion, a true contrarian is a person who understands that investors tend to overreact to both good and bad news, influenced by the media and experts. Contrarian investors always go against the prevailing mood. When everyone else is buying aggressively, the contrarian is quietly selling. When other investors are in a selling frenzy, the contrarian is picking up bargains. Contrarians believe that the best opportunities come during market extremes. Confidence in the contrarian philosophy and patience are essential to becoming a successful contrarian.

Unlike the poor sap I met at Harrah's who lost a nice profit because he had assumed the young man who had bet on the same horse he liked was a loser, we know whom to follow when it comes to picking stocks. In Chapter 5, I say that the majority of insiders are value investors. All Value Insiders are contrarians. Think about it. If a stock is depressed and out of favor, who would find it of value? Certainly not the momentum investor who will not be interested in the stock until it is in a clearly defined up trend, usually at a much higher price. That is why knowing what corporate insiders are doing in a depressed stock with contrarian potential is so important. Without insider buying, the bad news surrounding the stock is most likely justified, and a contrarian strategy based just on the fact that a stock is depressed will give you a loss, not a low risk buying opportunity.

Clearly, when it comes to picking individual stocks, you need to know what the masses are doing, but it is also essential you know what the informed minority is doing. By understanding the role of insider behavior in out of favor stocks, you truly can be an intelligent contrarian when it comes to stock picking.

Picking individual stocks is bottom-up or "micro" investing. Knowing when to be in the market or out at any give time is "macro" investing. It is just like when you are picking stocks. To be a successful contrarian, you need to know what the masses are doing relative to what the informed minority is doing. Most novice contrarians are like the bettor I referred to earlier. They assume the masses are always wrong. Nothing can be further from the truth. The masses are often right, especially during trends. It is at the extremes that they fail badly and that is when the true, intelligent contrarian shines and makes his or her monetary killing.

If you have read this far in my book, I assume you are a contrarian, either new or reinforced by my book. We are an eclectic bunch, not shackled by logic and facts. We know that contrary thinking is a right-brain activity and is truly an art form.

A subscriber to my Magic T service asked me if The Vital Few versus The Trivial Many contrarian philosophies could help with real estate investing. I have never owned real estate, other than the homes I lived in, but I am sure one could figure out what the informed professional real estate investors are doing versus what the public is doing.

In late 1978, I was living in South Florida and real estate prices were booming. I was playing tennis with a good friend from New York. He was very successful in real estate. I was a stockbroker then but since my friend rarely bought stocks and I knew nothing about real estate investing, we usually talked about sports and family issues.

After a game of singles, we took a break for lunch and sat in the middle of a group of men and women who were also taking a lunch break. One of the ladies to our right was a bit loud. I did not pay much attention to what she was talking about but the general drift was that she was a real estate broker and making a lot of money. Shortly after we had sat down, my friend left the table, and I saw him talking quietly on the nearby pay phone.

While we were walking to our court for a game of doubles, I asked him whom he had called. We were both single at the time and I assumed he had lined up a date for the weekend. He told me that he had called his attorney who handles all of his real estate investing and had instructed him to sell everything but the two homes my friend lived in, one in New York and the other in Miami.

I asked him why he had sold. He told me that he had been concerned for months over the escalated prices of his real estate investments and had been thinking about cutting back. He told me that the trigger for him to sell everything was the behavior of the lady at lunch. He said, "If this woman is making the kind of money she is talking about, given what I know about what a person with her qualifications should earn, that makes me absolutely sure we are at or very close to a top in real estate."

I was amazed and gratified. My friend was a contrarian investor, like me, just in a different field. He had his Vital Few and his Trivial Many. He knew value, was sophisticated, and understood that nature does not allow the masses to win at extremes. He had never read about Vilfredo Pareto, but he was a disciple, nevertheless. Five years later, my friend bought most of the real estate he had sold, for 50 cents on the dollar!

Investing in stocks comes with risk, and although having a sound strategy such as the Magic T can reduce the risk, it will never be eliminated. All investments have risk; even safe investments such as short-term U.S. government bills have the risk of inflation.

For contrarian investors, the major risk we must face is the chance of opportunity lost. While we sit on the sidelines because the market is soaring, driven by irrational exuberance, we are dealing with lost opportunity risk. Of course, losing an opportunity to make money is not the same as losing it. I have always been amused when I hear a money manager tell the media that the risk to investors is being out of the market at some given point in time, such as in mid-2000. What money managers fear is that they will be canned if the market keeps going up and they are not in it. Clearly, money managers have the risk of losing their great jobs, but in a rising market investors only face lost opportunity risk. Nobody is going to fire us if we are not in the stock market and it is climbing. We know that another low-risk opportunity is around the corner, and as usual, it will occur with irrational despair.

It is not the risk of opportunity lost that concerns me most; rather, it is the emotional pain that you may experience when the stock market moves in the opposite direction. This emotional anguish is usually highest just before you are going to be right. My fear is that new contrarians will give in to the unfamiliar emotional pain and jump into the prevailing trend at the wrong time. That is why it is important to believe in the contrarian system and prepare yourself for the type of emotional pain you may experience at extreme points in the stock market when the masses or Trivial Many are going against The Vital Few.

Sometimes, as a contrarian, you will feel lonely, especially at market turning points, dealing with the emotional pain and insecurity that accompany going against the grain of popular opinion.

I recently discovered a web site that I have found interesting and useful. It is the web site for the Contrarian Investing Association at www.contrarian-investing.com. Its goal is to bring independent-minded individuals together, share ideas, and make money while going against the masses. It is free, and you might find it helpful and enjoyable.

In my opinion, the intelligent application of contrarian principles will always work. I believe it is a law of nature and find it hard to discover any person of wealth and success who was not a contrarian at heart. Pareto's 80:20 principle is now more than 150 years old. Thirty years ago, when I became a contrarian investor, public opinion was shaped primarily by newspapers and magazines. A great clue to market tops and bottoms came from the cover of *Time* magazine. Snorting bulls appeared at market tops and growling bears at bottoms. Now we have a proliferation of financial programs such as Bloomberg, CNBC, Fox, and CNN to add to the collective chatter. As I stated in my introduction, being an intelligent contrarian has never been easier, and I expect this to continue for as long as there is free speech in this country.

For those who worry that too many people will adopt contrarianism, which will negate its effectiveness as a market strategy, I say "Forget it, never!" Right-brain activity is simply not a majority function. To be an intelligent contrarian, one has to think as an artist. Artists are in the minority of all society and since being a contrarian is an art form, we will always be in the minority.

Finally, there is another reason why The Vital Few versus The Trivial Many contrarian philosophy will have a minority of followers. It is a fact that my Magic T concept requires the willingness and the patience to wait for low-risk buying opportunities. Let me ask you a question; how many of your friends and acquaintances have patience? Check out people waiting in line at stores. Do they look rushed or relaxed? How about our roads and highways; are they littered with drivers obeying speed limits or are most in a hurry? I think you get my drift. Most people have little patience, and without it, you cannot be a contrarian investor. It is that simple.

CHAPTER 13

The Magic T: The Complete Strategy for Making Consistent Money in the Stock Market

By now, you already know how to be a consistent winner in the stock market. My strategy is simple, yet very sophisticated. The key is your willingness to follow the system and invest in the stock market only when the odds are with you. You will need to accept it that friends may tease you when you tell them you have been sitting on the sidelines, knowing they are in and are making money. Remember, most of your friends will be losers in the stock market because they are following The Trivial Many. When they tell you that you are a dinosaur, remember the story about my one-day golfing experience with the accountant.

The steps you must follow are:

1. Draw a T on a piece of lined paper, writing Buy on the left side and Stay Out on the right.

2. Write the word Insider in the column matching what the current insider position is.

3. Advisory Sentiment is a reverse indicator, so if it is positive, write Advisory Sentiment on the right side of the T. The Mood of the Media is also a reverse indicator. If most of what you hear or read is bearish, write Media in the left column.

4. Observing your friend's and the public's moods, write their status on the appropriate side of the T. This group is part of The Trivial Many so again, it is a reverse indicator.

5. Finally, write the State of the Market in one of the two columns. It too is a reverse indicator since it is influenced by The Trivial Many. If the market is oversold, then write it on the left or Buy side of the line.

Please review carefully the examples of the Magic T in Chapter 14. They will help you when it comes time for you to create your own. (For those of you who prefer that I do it for you, you can subscribe to my Magic T weekly report. Check out www.magict.info.)

All of the Magic T indicators dealing with sentiment are reverse indicators; therefore, you want to do the opposite of what the indicators are telling you to do. The only indicator that is standard is the Insider indicator. Insiders are The Vital Few and all others are The Trivial Many.

One might ask: In an ideal world, what would we like to see that would give us great confidence that we are forming a major economic and stock market bottom? Our answer would be: (1) heavy insider buying, (2) extreme investor pessimism based on negative Advisory Sentiment, (3) large mutual fund cash positions, (4) deeply oversold stock market, and (5) an extreme panic sell-off into the deeply oversold condition accompanied by a very negative news event.

The beautiful part of following The Vital Few is that there will be at least a few months' lead time prior to a tradable or secular bottom. At least once a year, you will have the opportunity to make a low-risk entry into the stock market, and every two or three years, you will have a major money making buying opportunity.

When your investment Magic T screams BUY, it is important that you remember that the buy signal will go against prevailing thought. I assure you that most market letter writers will be advising you to stay out of the market. You can also expect that CNBC, Bloomberg, and CNN will be interviewing bearish analysts, many of them long-time pathological bears. It is only human nature that you will question yourself. When this happens, you must look at the parade of negativism as proof that you are right.

If you follow the Magic T strategy, I guarantee two things: (1) it will work if you follow it, and (2) you will take emotional pain while you wait. I wish I could figure out a way to shorten the time between the Buy and Stay Out periods.

The problem is that to buy in at the bottom or sell out at the top, you have to be early. This is due to the fact that The Vital Few are Value Insiders who buy stocks as they drop and sell as they rise. Unlike money managers who are judged by their performance, they know they have a job and time on their hands, and, of course, nobody to answer to. They just keep working and buying stocks as the price of their company's stock declines. They know that eventually value will win out and they will make a lot of money in their stock.

When their stocks are rising, they sell and since most get stock options, they know they will have more stock to sell should stocks continue up. They also know that at some time in the future the stock market will allow them to get back in at favorable value points.

Some of my more seasoned followers understand the lead time associated with any contrarian strategy and use technical analysis to help them shorten the lead times. These investors know that my contrarian signal will be first and when they get a technical signal subsequent to the Magic T and it is in the same direction, they act fast, believing strongly that they will not be whipsawed. For those of you familiar with technical signals, it might be a good idea to use these signals in conjunction with the Magic T.

The following are the general guidelines that I use with the Magic T under all circumstances regardless of the technical picture:

Magic T—Stay Out (All five ingredients are on the right side.) Do not buy stocks, including those with positive insider patterns, during times when the Magic T's five inputs are all in the Stay Out pattern. For those with experience on the short side, you can short stocks with negative insider patterns. Stocks with insider selling into price weakness are especially valuable as shorts. Technical analysis can be useful for timing short sales.

Magic T—Neutral (Ingredients are mixed, not all on the same side.) When the Magic T is in the neutral phase, focus on selecting stocks with neutral or positive insider buying. For short sellers, choose stocks with negative insider patterns that are already in downtrends. Use primarily a trading strategy for both longs and shorts. Technical analysis can be useful for timing of buying and selling longs and shorts. If short-term trading is not your style, my advice is to stay on the sidelines and be patient.

Magic T—Buy (All five ingredients are on the left side.) When the Magic T's five ingredients are in the Buy mode, I would recommend buying stocks with neutral or positive insider patterns. It would be a mistake to short during a Magic T Buy. Technical analysis is not necessary since many of the most attractive stocks will have ugly chart patterns.

Each person has to decide what level of comfort and patience he or she has when it comes to the stock market. Chapter 2 points out the importance of having a strategy, preferably top down. My strategy is to buy stocks aggressively when the Magic T is in the Buy mode. When the Magic T is in the Stay Out mode, I use about 20 percent of my funds for shorting exchange traded index funds, especially the SPDR (symbol SPY) that mirrors the price movement of the Standard & Poor's 500. When the Magic T is neutral, I use about 30 percent of my capital to trade stocks long only, taking profits quickly and using close stops.

Conservative investors could simply buy a combination of no-load value and growth equity mutual funds when the Magic T flashes a Buy signal and then sell and move the proceeds to money market funds when the Magic T changes to the Stay Out mode.

You need guts and money at intermediate and major bottoms. I assure you that you will have both if you believe in The Vital Few versus The Trivial Many concepts and follow them.

Good fortune.

CHAPTER 14

Examples of
the Magic T in Action

ON FEBRUARY 21, 2001, I CREATED THE FOLLOWING MAGIC T AS PART
of my regular weekly stock market review, which prompted this
bearish memo to my clients.

Buy	*Stay Out*
	Insiders—Bearish
	Advisory Sentiment—Bullish
	Mood of the Media—Bullish
	Mood of Friends and Acquaintances—Bullish
	State of the Market—Overbought

Memo to Clients

Last month, I recommended that you view the market as a trading affair and not the beginning of a new secular uptrend. In June, I downgraded the stock market to neutral from an insider perspective and recommended stock selectivity as the key to survival. With insiders now negative, I recommend an even more defensive posture at this time. Almost 60 percent of all market advisors are bullish. Last week, I heard a well-regarded analyst on CNBC say, "This is the best buying opportunity of a decade." Everyone is entitled to his or her opinion. However, I must disagree with that statement.

(Dow Jones Average—10,691)

On July 19, 2002, my regular weekly stock market review using the Magic T resulted in a market upgrade, prompting another memo.

Buy

Advisory Sentiment—Bearish

Mood of the Media—Bearish

Mood of Friends and Acquaintances—Bearish

State of the Market—Oversold

Stay Out

Insiders—Neutral

Memo to Clients

Insiders are now neutral on the stock market. Meanwhile, investment advisory services are more bearish than bullish. Also, in the eyes of many technicians, the market has become very oversold. I would be remiss not to point out that a strong market rally could occur at any time under these conditions. I believe the ultimate bottom will occur when we see aggressive insider buying. In my opinion, any rallies from current levels are strictly for traders. Since insider selling started drying up in the April to June period, insiders will be allowed to buy back in the fourth quarter, which is why I still believe the true market bottom will occur in the fourth quarter.

(Dow Jones Average—8,668)

The July 19, 2002, prediction of a market bottom in October was prophetic. On October 10, 2002, my weekly stock market review turned fully bullish and, with the aid of the Magic T, caused me to issue this positive memo to my clients.

Buy   *Stay Out*

Insiders—Bullish

Advisory Sentiment—Bearish

Mood of the Media—Bearish

Mood of Friends—Bearish

State of the Market—Oversold

Memo to Clients

I expect a strong market until mid-February for the following reasons: First, insiders are positive. Second, last week the number of market newsletters that were positive (28 percent) was the lowest in eight years and the number of bearish letters (43 percent) was the highest in four years. The reality of bearish investor sentiment against a background of bullish insider activity is hard to ignore and forms the basis of my short-term bullishness. As I stated last month, the level of insider buying does not support a major secular low

at this time. However, we will deal with that issue early next year. For now, I advise buying favored stocks and recommend hedge funds maintain a net long bias.
(Dow Jones Average—7,534)

On March 7, 2003, the Magic T gave its third consecutive positive reading as the market made a triple bottom in the Dow 7,500 area. I changed the format for the newsletter that week and the following was sent out.

Buy   *Stay Out*

Insiders

Advisory Sentiment

State of the Market

Mood of the Media

Mood of Friends et al.

Vital Few

Insiders are bullish as they are buying nearly as much as they are selling, compared to their normal level of 2-1 selling to buying.

Trivial Many

Advisory Sentiment—Bears at 38 percent, the highest in 10 weeks

State of the Market—Lowry's overbought/oversold indicator is the most oversold in 37 years

Mood of the Media—Watch CNBC for two hours and you will quickly become deeply depressed

Examples of the Magic T in Action

Mood of Friends, et al.—At a recent book fair, when I mentioned my stock market book, I was treated as if I had leprosy.

Conclusion

We have a deeply oversold market with growing investor and media pessimism, and insiders are buying. It is too early to advise that we have made THE bottom; however, this is clearly a low risk entry point, at least for the next few months.

The August 30, 2003, Magic T is a good example of the type of emotional pain one must take from time to time when you follow a contrarian strategy, no matter how sophisticated it might be. The Magic T flashed great buy signals in July and October 2002 and March 2003. Remember my contrarian motto "Bought Well—Half Sold." We certainly bought well, but getting out of the stock market in August 2003 was very early since the stock market did not top out until the first week in January. Six months is a long time. Of course, when you are on the sidelines after having made a nice profit in your previous low-risk investments, you are not losing money. You are just not making any; in effect, you are suffering an opportunity loss. Nevertheless, without a lot of experience with contrarian investing, the emotional pain you take can be upsetting for many investors. I went through it in 1973–1974, 1987, 2000, and again in 2003. In all previous cases, my faith in the Magic T paid off and I always marvel at how smart I feel after the market crashes and I have loads of cash to put to work at the next bottom. Just the same, it is not fun to sit on the sidelines and wait while the world has seemingly conspired to make you feel stupid.

The Vital Few versus The Trivial Many

The August 30, 2003, report was sent and the level of the Dow Jones Industrials was 9,415.

Buy	Stay Out
	Insiders
	Advisory Sentiment
	State of the Market
	Mood of the Media
	Friends, et al.

The Vital Few

Insider selling in August continued the negative trend seen since June. As expected, insider sell/buy ratios across all indexes and market caps sizes have peaked. Insider selling in most stocks peaked in the May–June period. In the past, the next buy signal of the Magic T had occurred six months after insider selling hit highs and started to recede. That would put the next low-risk entry point for the stock market in the fourth quarter.

The Trivial Many

Advisory Sentiment—Far too many bullish advisors. The number of bearish experts is very low, similar to levels seen at most market tops in the past 40 years.

State of the Market—Still overbought. At our March 12 Buy signal, only 6 percent of Dow stocks were in uptrends versus 80 percent currently. At the next bottom, this ratio should be in the 30 percent range. It peaked at 90 percent in early June. A further decline to below 70 percent would be a sell signal for this indicator.

Examples of the Magic T in Action

Mood of the Media—Very upbeat as every report is viewed through rose-colored glasses. High unemployment, no problem, productivity is better. High gas prices, no problem, consumers don't care, they will drive anyway and besides Europe drivers pay more. Huge deficits, no problem, it is only a small percent of GDP.

Mood of Friends, et al.—Money from the public is flowing into mutual funds. The fund managers must be fully invested so this money gets into stocks pushing them higher. To keep up with their peers in the performance game, they must buy overvalued stocks simply because that is where the action is.

Conclusion

Risk remains very high for new stock purchases. Keep an eye on existing positions and place stops to protect your holdings. Avoid laggard stocks that have 40 percent or more of institutional ownership. The low-risk approach to year-end buying is discussed in Addendum B of my new book: If we get the decline I expect, the profits gleaned in a four-month hold could make for a profitable year.

Special Note: Chapter 13 discussed how many of our institutional clients use technical analysis to shorten the lead times of the Magic T when it turns to the Stay Out phase. If you have trouble being patient during the occasional long lead times, you should try adding some market timing indicators.

Combining George Soros' Reflexivity Theory with The Vital Few versus The Trivial Many

THE QUANTUM FUND, RUN BY GEORGE SOROS AND STANLEY Druckenmiller, was a client of my consulting company for 10 years. When their fund closed in 2001, I retained Stan and six of the seven general partners when they went on their own. One of these partners subsequently bought my firm, Muzea Insider Consulting Services, and I have remained as president, specializing in top-down analysis to form the monthly macro picture.

I have been intrigued by George Soros since 1987 after reading his book *Alchemy of Finance*. He is one of the most brilliant people of our times, and I am a believer in his theory of "reflexivity." On September 16, 2002, George Soros was interviewed on CNBC's *After Hours* program. I have been interviewed many times on television and have learned that most interviewers have their own agenda. This causes them to ignore interesting clues that the person being interviewed offers, which is exactly what happened in the Soros interview. Rather than following the lead that Soros offered concerning his theory of reflexivity, the interviewer asked his opinion of oil stocks.

After the interview, I reflected on the theory of reflexivity that Soros had created and believe his theory actually adds credence to my own theory of The Vital Few versus The Trivial Many. Reflexivity is a two-way feedback mechanism in which reality shapes a participant's thinking, and the participant's thinking helps shape reality in an unending process.

In the stock market, the theory of reflexivity states that the participant's bias can change the fundamentals, which then determine market prices. This bias usually occurs in every boom and bust cycle or stock market bubble. The participant's views and the actual state of affairs may be mutually self-reinforcing at first. However, the thought process is bound to become unsustainable in the long run, ultimately causing a move in the opposite direction. The trick, of course, is to be aware of this unsustainability and to know when to act on it. You must look for a catalyst that will start a move to the opposite direction.

For example, in 1992, Soros and everyone else who followed currency trends knew that the British government was going to raise interest rates to protect their currency. Soros, however, correctly reasoned that the United Kingdom's economy was slowing down and that raising interest rates would weaken it more. He had his catalyst to act. In effect, the U.K.'s actions to defend the Sterling were unsustainable and his bet against their currency made him $2 billion.

George Soros' Reflexivity Theory

My theory of The Vital Few versus The Trivial Many is similar in that I know it is impossible for the masses to be right at major turning points. They can be right for a while since they are acting on their beliefs, which reinforces the existing trend. Ultimately though, when they have all acted, the reverse has to occur. When The Trivial Many have all acted, while at the same time The Vital Few have taken an opposite position, the trend must reverse. It is just a matter of time.

In October 2002, there were many negative events: global terrorism, threat of war with Iraq, dock strikes in California, corporate scandals, growing deficits, and so on. With the constant reporting of this negativity by the media, the market trend continued down, aided by professional program trading. Since I knew that the stock market was deeply oversold, the real fact of the stock market was that most of the bad news was already in the market. The level of bearish market letter writers was at the highest point in four years and insiders were buying. I knew the decline was unsustainable but needed a clue to act on. The clue occurred on October 10, when the stock market rallied with no good news. That was my catalyst. It was a clue to me that institutional investors saw great value in the market at the beaten down prices. Clearly, most of The Trivial Many had sold and the supply of stocks would dry up dramatically. Once the market trend had reversed, I knew that the same investors, such as program traders who were driving the market lower, would soon be aiding the market on the upside.

It was then that I was able to combine reflexivity with The Vital Few. My theory got me prepared to act and George Soros' theory taught me to look for clues as to when to act. I look for-

APPENDIX A

For Short Sellers (Handle with Caution)

I HAVE BEEN ADVISING HEDGE FUNDS FOR 14 YEARS WITH NEW IDEAS to short stocks. If you have never shorted a stock, than I suggest you avoid this section. If you understand the pitfalls and have shorted stocks before, then read on.

Most professionals and the public who short stocks seem to get involved with the same names. Maybe there is comfort in groups when it comes to making bets that a stock will collapse. When a stock does collapse, most short sellers are elated because they have huge profits and they can brag to their peers, especially those they know whom were hurt because they were long (or buying).

Unfortunately, most stocks that are clearly overvalued and popular shorts among hedge funds are usually in strong up trends. I have seen many short side managers forced to cover because the stocks kept getting more overvalued, only to collapse after they had bought the shares back. This is a double whammy and very damaging to the fund manager's ego and their client's pocket.

My advice is simple. Look for stocks that are in well-established downtrends, especially those that have stopped going down and are moving sideways. Then check Yahoo!'s Finance section and click on the Insider link or go to the Washington Service. Look to see if insiders sold at higher price levels and are now selling at lower levels, especially if they had not sold for a few months while the stock was moving sideways. If they start selling again at lower levels, that usually means whatever problems they are having that caused the stock to drop are still occurring.

The first price drop loses the momentum investors. The second drop, after additional bad news, will lose value investors. With no one left to support it, the stock will drop suddenly and continue to drift lower.

Some of the best shorts I have provided my clients over the past two years had similar characteristics. Enron, Micron Technology, Juniper Networks, Siebel Systems, and many more were all huge short-side winners and all had insider selling into price weakness.

You might become a believer in no time at all.

For Investors Who Like to Buy Stock Bottoms

MOST INVESTORS, ESPECIALLY TECHNICIANS, WILL LAUGH IF YOU TELL them you are a bottom fisher in the stock market. It can be done, even when the stock market is in a downtrend and The Vital Few versus The Trivial Many are telling us to Stay Out. Of course, it works better when our contrarian strategy is screaming Buy.

This concept is called Tax Loss Buys. It is only practiced in October of each year. You buy beaten down stocks in mid-October and sell them no later than mid-February the following year, which means this is, at best, a four-month trading strategy. Your goal is to achieve an 18 to 26 percent return. Whenever I achieve these returns before the normal four-month period is up, I take my profits. I recommend you do so as well.

To find these Tax Loss Buys, purchase *Barron's* on the first Monday in October. Turn to the section New Highs and Lows. Then find the new lows on the New York Stock Exchange (NYSE). This is a list of all stocks that hit 52-week lows the previous week. You will need either a Stock Guide or Value Line, or you can use the Yahoo! Finance site, to get the symbols. Then follow these steps:

1. For every stock, subtract the company's current liabilities from their current assets. If there is a residual number, then subtract the figure for the company's long-term debt. If there is no residual number, cross the stock off your list. You must have a positive value after subtracting the short- and the long-term debt from current assets or the stock does not qualify.

2. Go into BigCharts.com and look at the 10-year chart of each remaining stock. If the stock is not in the lower third of a 10-year price history, cross it out.

3. Check Yahoo! or Value Line to see what percentage of institutional ownership there is. The minimum number is 30 percent.

4. Go into Yahoo! Finance again, reviewing the stock's latest news to see if the company is earning money, even a penny. If it is currently in the red or its last quarterly earnings report was in the red, cross it off.

If you start with 100 stocks on the NYSE New Low List, you will probably have no more than 10 stocks that qualify. These 10 stocks, however, will be the only companies with strong balance sheets and current earnings. The stocks will also be in the bottom range of a 10-year price history, faced with institutional tax loss selling that must be completed by October 31. Determine your total investment amount and buy equal dollars of all the qualified stocks, and sell them all in mid-February.

For Investors Who Like to Buy Stock Bottoms

I have used this strategy for 25 years and made money every year, except one. In 1981, I broke even when the market collapsed in January. It is a great once-a-year investing strategy and one that will align you with The Vital Few. In this strategy, you will often see insiders buying in general as they often do in October.

Give it a try. There are very few times on Wall Street when you have such an edge.

APPENDIX C

For Investors
Who Do Not Want
to Buy Only Stocks

IN ADDITION TO BUYING INDIVIDUAL STOCKS WHEN THE MAGIC T IS screaming Buy, you can also consider mutual funds and exchange-traded funds.

Mutual funds pool the money of people with similar investment goals, such as increasing current income, maximizing long-term growth, or combining growth and income. Professional investment managers use the money to buy securities of companies that they believe will best achieve the investors' objectives. When you buy shares in a mutual fund, you are buying a proportionate share of ownership in the collective portfolio. Some of what the fund earns may be passed along to you periodically in the form of dividends and capital gains distributions. The rest of the investment earnings increases the value of outstanding shares.

If you sell your shares at a price higher than you paid for them, you will realize a capital gain. If you sell at a lower price than you paid, you will have a capital loss. People without the resources to amass broadly diversified portfolios on their own—much less the time and expertise it takes to manage them effectively—find investing in mutual funds a good strategy.

Investors with more time and expertise might want to consider exchange-traded funds. These are index funds that are listed on the American Stock Exchange and can be traded during the day. Each fund has a single security designed to track the collective performance of its respective index. There are more than 100 exchange traded funds to choose from.

The ones I trade most often are SPDRs and QQQs. SPDRs (symbol SPY) mirror the price movement of the Standard & Poor's 500. The S&P 500 has most of the biggest companies and if I am right on the overall trend of the stock market, I will make money. I used to trade regular S&P 500 Index funds through my brokers, but there are two disadvantages. The first is that you have to wait until the close of business trading to buy and I like to buy during the day, especially on a price dip. The second is an early redemption fee, approximately three-quarters of a percent, if you sell before six months has elapsed. I want more flexibility than that and do not like throwing my money away on an extra fee, especially when the exchange-traded funds provide the same result and can be bought and sold during the day for a discount commission. The QQQs mirror the price movement of the 100 largest nonfinancial stocks on the NASDAQ. Since many of these stocks are in the technology sector, I trade this fund only when I am positive on this sector.

You can get all the information on exchange-traded funds on the web site amex.com. Check them out; they are exciting new vehicles.

APPENDIX D

Tweaking the Magic T

OVER THE YEARS, I HAVE GROWN ACCUSTOMED TO WORKING WITH institutional investors, especially hedge fund managers. These professionals use a variety of strategies to pick stocks and judge market risk. Most are value investors, using a broad array of tools to measure value. Some of these fundamental attributes are a growth of earnings per share, stock price in relation to stated book value, return on equity, and stock momentum.

Muzea Insider Consulting Services provides these money managers with insider trading analysis on those stocks we monitor for them, clues as to which sectors and industries insiders favor or disfavor, and aggregate analysis of insider behavior to help them judge certain stocks and market risk.

It is easy to work with these professionals because I know we are just one piece of information they consider in making both micro (stocks) and macro (big picture) decisions. I understand, for example, that when our aggregate analysis of market risk differs from theirs, they will ignore our input and rely on their own. Working with professional money managers, I know that we get no blame or glory with our micro and macro calls.

Since our clients pull the trigger, they get all the glory or the blame.

When I made the decision to help individual investors in early 2003, I knew it would be in the best interest of the individual investor for me to keep my contrarian philosophy simple and easy to follow. At the request of some readers, I decided to start an inexpensive subscription service to provide a weekly Magic T, the technique I use to clearly describe market risk.

My original book was published in February 2003, and my individual subscription service began in August of that year. Providing this service has helped me discover the differences between giving advice to individual investors versus institutional money managers. The main difference is the average individual investor does not have anywhere near the resources that the professional investor has.

Two or three times a decade, when the market is in a very strong up trend driven by momentum investors, most sentiment indicators will fail. Since the Magic T uses sentiment as one of its key ingredients, during these strong momentum up trends the Magic T will be in the Stay Out phase. This is what happened in the spring of 1987 and late summer of 2003. In 1987, the Magic T moved to Stay Out in April but the market did not crash until October. As of this writing, the market topped out in January 2004, six months after the Magic T had moved to Stay Out.

Some of my Magic T subscribers and all of my institutional clients know how to tweak the Magic T signals and understand the lead time associated with any contrarian strategy. They use technical analysis to help them shorten the lead times. These investors know that my contrarian signal will most often come first and when they get a technical signal subsequent to the Magic T, and it is in the same direction, they act fast, believing strongly that they will not be whipsawed. If their technical signal precedes the Magic T, their confidence increases.

To give some insights as to how to blend the Magic T with technical analysis, I asked my good friend, Mike Hurley, to address this issue. Mike is a Chartered Market Technician and 20-year stock market veteran. His research has been widely followed and frequently quoted throughout the financial media. He currently publishes his research independently, and manages money based on his proprietary market timing methods. Mike can be reached at mike@mikehurley.com. His article, entitled "Technical Analysis: Where the Rubber Meets the Road," follows:

What Is Technical Analysis?

While quite well known in the financial industry, the field of technical analysis is equally misunderstood. Some consider the tools and setups so reliable they have earned names such as the Holy Grail or Kiss of Death patterns, while others consider them no better than snake oil or voodoo. The truth of course, is somewhere in the middle, and largely dependent on the skill of the practitioner. Just as there is a Mozart, Gretzky, and Einstein, some folks are far more proficient at reading charts than others.

Charts are at the heart of technical analysis, the earliest of which date back to the rice pits of Osaka, Japan, in the early 1600s. From those beginnings, the field has grown in both popularity and esteem, and now offers a professional designation like many others. Additional information on the Chartered Market

Technician (CMT) program can be found at www.mta.org, but for now, let us just look at how technical tools can help us with our timing decisions.

How Does Technical Analysis Work?

The most unique feature of technical analysis is that it focuses exclusively on market-based information. This is why some of its practitioners are titled Market Analyst or Chief Market Strategist. Obviously, we are all limited to only two ways in which we can express our viewpoint in the marketplace, either as a buy order or a sell order. Period. If there are more buy orders than sell orders, prices will rise. If the sellers are more numerous and/or more aggressive than the buyers, prices will fall. This is true for stocks, bonds, commodities, options, gold, diamonds, homes, cars, everything. So while all analysts use the same basic rules of economics when looking at stocks, the technical analyst differs from the fundamental analyst in that he or she measures the *supply and demand* for the pieces of paper that are traded, as opposed to the *goods or services* the company provides.

The theory behind technical analysis then is that all the information and knowledge that exists, be it public, or nonpublic, is reflected in the balance between supply and demand and it is this balance that determines the direction of prices. In the strictest sense, the technician does not care whether the supply or demand comes from The Vital Few or The Trivial Many. That being said, both The Vital Few and Trivial Many are important groups to monitor, and it is often said that "charts show the footprints of the smart money."

The Tools of Technical Analysis

The tools technicians use fall into several basic categories: charts, indicators, market internals, sentiment, and intermarket relationships. Charts are clearly the most basic reflection of supply and demand, and as they say, a picture is truly worth a thousand words! Being visual, charts can be interpreted rather easily, something that has in large part contributed to their popularity. The easiest and most basic way to understand a chart is to look for levels where tops and bottoms seem to form consistently. For example, let us say XYZ rallies up to $40, and then gets turned away. We could then easily deduce that $40 is where the balance of supply and demand shifted, and where the supply of the sellers overcame the demand of buyers. Now let us say XYZ holds at $35, and makes another run at $40 and again fails to get through that level. We would then see a chart with two separate and distinct tops at $40, which would literally show us that 40 was an area of resistance. For the sake of argument, let us say that XYZ holds at $35 several times as well. This would then be termed an area of support for the stock.

These areas of support and resistance are among the easiest things to spot on a chart, and are very important to technicians for several reasons. First of all, knowing where support and resistance are helps us in entering positions. After all, if $35 is support on XYZ, why buy up at $38? Why not save a few bucks and get it at $35? Another, and arguably more valuable use of support and resistance to long-term investors, is to know when they break. For example, if XYZ has been getting turned away consistently at $40, wouldn't it be important if the stock got through that area? Absolutely, and this is what technicians call a "breakout." In fact, while this may not seem intuitive, the most bullish thing a stock can do is to break to a new all-time high.

While it seems that the stock would be too expensive to buy, the truth of the matter is that there are no natural sellers or areas of resistance overhead. A very bullish situation indeed!

Now, wouldn't it be valuable if we could combine this concept with what The Vital Few might be telling us? This certainly makes sense. Let us look at a quick example.

After a brutal decline, which lasted more than two years and took the stock from nearly $83 to $2.50, Nextel (NXTL) finally found a bottom in June 2002. The stock rallied sharply through the rest of the year, before hitting resistance in the $14.50 area. (See Figure D.1.) Although it could be argued that the stock was expensive, particularly compared to where it had just been, a catalytic insider of Nextel made a significant purchase in March 2003. This was clearly a bullish sign, but still no guarantee that the stock was headed higher. However, wouldn't it be a good sign if Nextel could break out? Wouldn't that mean that all the sellers at that level had been absorbed, and that Nextel was in fact actually heading higher?

Yes, and while it might seem that paying $15 for Nextel would be too much, waiting for a breakout is actually a safer entry, as it lets the stock prove to us with its own actions that it is indeed ready to move higher. Nextel did in fact break out in May, and then really got going in June. By January the stock had doubled. (See Figure D.2.)

Another of the most basic technical tools, and one anyone can use, is the trendline. They are purely visual, and extremely easy to employ. To identify a downtrend, just draw a line across two or more tops. Two or more bottoms can be joined to define an up

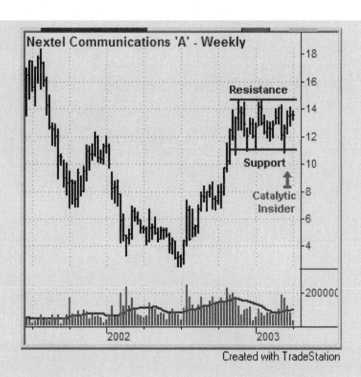

FIGURE D.1 Nextel Communications "A"—Weekly: Rally

trend. These lines are quite effective, and apply to any chart in any time frame. In the charts of the S&P 500 Index from late-1999 to mid-2000, you can see a picture-perfect uptrend line. When this line was violated in October 2000, it was a clear message from the market itself that stocks had finished going up.

The biggest mistake most people make when using trendlines is that they assume a new trend will ensue in the opposite direction. While this is, of course, one of the two options, it is entirely possible that the stock or the market will enter a sideways consolidation phase. While this may sound frustrating, it is often enough to know where a stock or the market is not headed. After

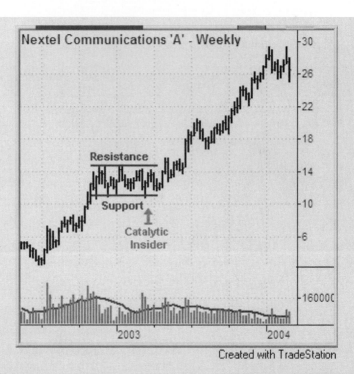

FIGURE D.2   Nextel Communications "A"—Weekly: Breakout

all, don't we endeavor to own stocks that are going up, but if a stock we own is no longer going up, do we really care whether it goes sideways or lower? Probably not. It is best to sell it, and find the next great opportunity.

In the chart shown in Figure D.3, the S&P 500 tried to stabilize in late-2000 after what many thought would be a standard 15 percent correction, creating a nice little dip to buy. Nothing could have been further from the truth however, and The Vital Few provided a valuable clue as to the risk that lay ahead. While, of course, no one person nor any group can ever know the future with any certainty, it *is* important when insiders are voting with

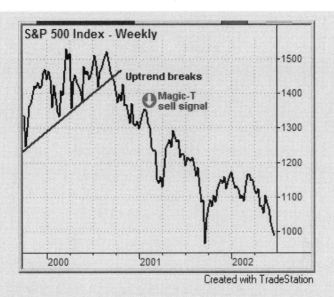

FIGURE D.3   S&P 500 Index—Weekly

their money. After all, if the people most in touch with their business see risk going forward, are we really in a position to argue? Should we instead trust the judgment of our brokers, or analysts who opine based on data, which reports the past? I do not think so. The market's opinion is the only one that matters, and when insiders are selling into weakness, as evidenced by a Magic T sell signal, we probably should be too.

Indicators

While basic chart analysis can be quite useful, and something literally anybody can do, technicians are most well known for their use of indicators. These are nothing more than mathematical studies and formulas that try to provide insight into the direction a market is most likely headed. Like any other specialized field, these studies can get quite complex, and really beyond the scope of our discussion here. Many investors however, including myself, have found these studies extremely useful and for those so inclined, I encourage you to find out more about them.

One of the most basic examples of a technical indicator is to smooth price by taking a moving average of it. In Figure D.4, we have added a 40-week (also known as a 200-day) moving average to the figure, which does indeed help us see the major trend. While some even use this indicator as a mechanical system for buying and selling when prices cross the moving average, this

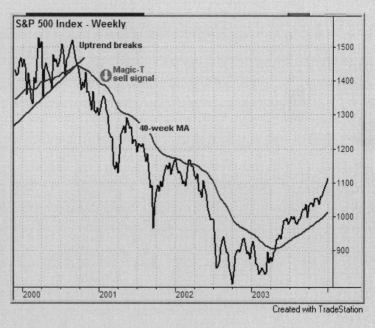

FIGURE D.4 S&P 500 Index—Weekly

strategy can lead to frequent whipsaws in a sideways market. In the hands of individual investors, the best tool is to use it as a way to confirm the market's trend. Continuing to use our example, once the market broke its up trend in October of 2000, we could comfortably say that stocks had most likely finished going up. Then when the Magic T flashed a sell signal in early 2001, it should have tempered any urge we had to buy stocks at what seemed to be cheap prices. The 40-week moving average confirmed the downtrend, and steered us away from entering the market until stocks had stabilized and had formed a base in early 2003.

Market Internals

Among the purest, most effectivetechnical tools ever conceived fall into a broad category called market internals. Much the way a doctor gauges the health of a patient by measuring vital signs such as pulse and blood pressure, the market technician can get a very good read on the health of the stock market by reviewing the number of stocks advancing and declining, as well as those scoring new highs and new lows. When market internals are in gear, and agree with the trend of the major averages, we can consider the trend to be healthy or intact. When these measures diverge from the major averages, then we should pay particular attention, as an important turning point may be near.

Expanding our review of the S&P 500, we see a classic example of how market internals can provide us a keen insight into the health of the stock market. (See Figure D.5.) Specifically, as stocks declined throughout 2001 and the first half of 2002 (A, B,

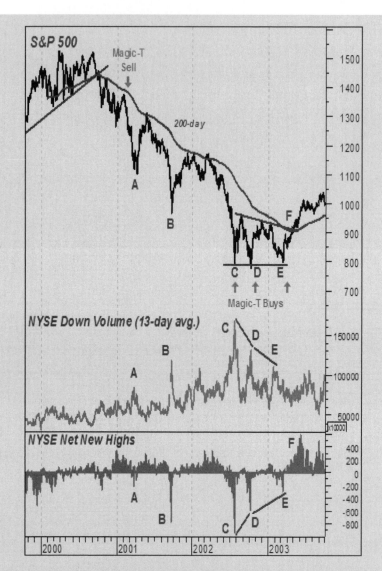

FIGURE D.5   S&P 500 and NYSE

Charts made with MetaStock® from Equis International, Inc.

and C), each new low in the S&P 500 was accompanied by an increase in both down volume and the number of stocks scoring new 52-week lows. Market internals clearly confirmed the downtrend and suggested that the best course of action was to stay away. Interestingly, The Vital Few found value in the market with the S&P at 800 in July 2002 (C), and the Magic T flashed a buy signal. Stocks bounced and then tested the 800 area in October, at which point insiders were back again buying. The difference this time, however, is that market internals formed two powerful divergences. Specifically, as the S&P went sideways from (C) to (D), the selling came on less down volume and fewer new 52-week lows. This successful test of the July lows was the first step in the rebuilding process and made stocks much more attractive from a technical perspective.

After failing at resistance in November 2002, the market again tested established support in the 800 area in March 2003 (E). This time the bears mustered even less down volume and fewer new lows, an indication that they were truly out of gas. For those who doubted and continued to fight the tape, the breakout in the S&P in May (F) was accompanied by the largest number of new 52-highs seen in years, a clear signal that stocks had finished going down.

Inter-Market Relationships

Another area of critical importance to many successful investors is that of inter-market relationships. While some consider this to be economic analysis, it is best thought of as technical as the inputs analyzed are real time and market based.

Wrapping up our review of the S&P 500, we can clearly see the market bottom of October 1998. Stocks surged off those lows, gaining 30 percent by January. In textbook fashion, the economic upturn put in motion a series of events that typically occur throughout the business cycle and offer those paying attention a series of signposts that evaluate the level of risk in the marketplace. The first was an increase in demand for raw materials, which caused crude oil to bottom in December 1998. Rising commodity prices are by definition inflation and something that puts pressure on interest rates. By early 1999, it was clear that long rates were indeed on the rise and over time, they dragged short rates with them. This is typical, as it is the Federal Reserve that controls short-term rates, and traditionally they are reacting to market pressures as opposed to creating them.

In early 2000, inflationary pressures had started to narrow the yield curve. (See Figure D.6.) This often occurs late in an expansion, as long-term rates, which are market driven, discount the future likelihood of inflation. With short rates aggressively on the rise, the bond market no longer saw inflation as a worry. This was enough to put a top on the NASDAQ, which occurred in March 2000. The Federal Reserve remained ever vigilant, however, and continued to raise the Fed Funds rate through May 16, 2000, to a rate of 6.5 percent and then held them there until January 2001. This extremely aggressive tight money policy caused the yield curve to invert, which is a term used to describe when short-term rates are actually higher than longer-term rates. The Fed held the curve inverted for a full six months, something several market analysts have called irresponsible, and dubbed the proximate cause for the severity of the economic conditions experienced as the new millenium unfolded. While that issue will be long de-

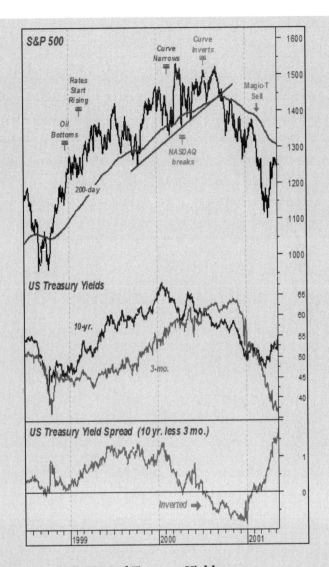

FIGURE D.6   S&P 500 and Treasury Yields
Charts Made with MetaStock® from Equis International, Inc.

bated, there is no doubt that an inverted yield curve is the single-most bearish economic omen known in the stock market. An inverted yield curve preceded the recessions of 1970, 1974, 1980, 1982, and 1990 as well as that of the new century. When the curve inverts, it is best to avoid stocks, period. Insiders clearly read that signpost and saw the difficult economic times ahead. Something that no doubt led to the Magic T sell signal in February 2001.

The bottom line is that the market's voice is the only one that matters, and when the market speaks, . . . it pays to listen!

Glossary

Advisory Sentiment Index   A survey of more than 140 independent (nonbrokerage house) stock market newsletters based
on the most recent advice to their subscribers. A high percentage
of bulls and a low percentage of bears occur as the markets form
a top, and a low percentage of bulls and a high percentage of
bears occur as the markets form a bottom. This is a contrary
opinion indicator. The more bears counted, the greater the upside potential; and the more bulls, the larger the risk of a steep
decline. Developed by Mike Burke of Chartcraft.

Bigcharts.com   Charting web site service providing free access
to charts, reports, indicators, and quotes for stocks, mutual
funds, and major market indices.

Bloomberg.com   Free financial web site providing data, quotes,
and news on the world's financial markets with up-to-the-
minute information on equities and mutual funds.

Bullish   A term for rising prices, derived from the bull, which
tosses his victims into the air when attacking.

Bearish   A term for declining prices, derived from the bear,
which claws his victims to the ground when attacking.

Chartcraft.com   Point-and-figure charting service of stocks,
indexes, and sectors. Also provides weekly advisory sentiment
and insider analysis for the contrarian investor.

CNBC   Financial television network offering live real-time coverage of U.S. stock markets.

CNN   One of the world's leaders in television news, including financial markets.

Divergence   A deviation from a previous path or plan.

80:20 Rule   Vilfredo Pareto's rule which states that a small number of causes is responsible for a large percentage of the effect, in a ratio of about 20:80. Expressed in a management context, 20 percent of a person's effort generates 80 percent of the person's results. The corollary to this is that 20 percent of one's results absorb 80 percent of one's resources or efforts.

Exchange traded funds   Baskets of securities similar to a mutual fund, designed to generally track a broad stock or bond index or an economic sector, yet trades like a single stock.

Hedge fund   Private investment partnership with management compensation tied to performance, generally 20 percent of the profits. The general partners usually invest their own capital as well. Most hedge fund managers have a great deal of flexibility in their investment options, especially in short sales.

Insider   Any officer or director of a publicly traded company who must file a change of ownership with the Securities and Exchange Commission (SEC). Any outsider who owns 10 percent or more of a public company is also an insider and must file with the SEC. Insider trades must be sent to the SEC within two days following the transaction.

Interactive reasoning   A reasoning process that requires the decision maker to interpret any single piece of information depending on how he evaluates many other inputs.

Glossary

Investment letter writers   Individuals who earn their living writing letters to subscribers advising them on the trend of the market, including stocks to buy or to short.

Linear reasoning   A reasoning process where our minds travel from one point to another in a logical sequence.

Magic T   A method of analyzing a major decision by removing emotions out of the reasoning process.

New Low List   Company stocks making new 52-week lows, broken down by exchange. The list can be found in the *Wall Street Journal* each day and in *Barron's* on Mondays.

New York Stock Exchange specialists   The NYSE uses an agency auction market system. Specialists make markets in stocks and work on the NYSE. The responsibility of a specialist is to make a fair and orderly market in the issues assigned to them. They must yield to public orders, which means they may not trade for their own account when there are public bids and offers. The specialist has an affirmative obligation to eliminate imbalances of supply and demand when they occur. NYSE specialists have large capital requirements.

QQQ   An Exchange Traded Fund that trades like a stock and mirrors the price movement of the 100 largest nonfinancial stocks on the NASDAQ.

Short sales   The selling of a security that the seller does not own, or any sale that is completed by the delivery of a security borrowed by the seller. Short sellers assume the risk that they will be able to buy the stock at a lower amount than the price at which they sold short.

SPDR   An Exchange Traded Fund that trades like a stock and mirrors the price movement of the Standard & Poor's 500 Composite Stock Price Index.

Standard & Poors 500   Regarded as the standard for measuring large-cap U.S. stock market performance, this popular index includes a representative sample of leading companies in leading industries. The S&P 500 is used by 97 percent of U.S. money managers and pension plan sponsors. More than $1 trillion is indexed to the S&P 500.

Tax loss buy candidates   A list of depressed stocks with strong balance sheets and good long-term prospects that are experiencing tax loss selling by institutions and individuals, usually compiled in the fourth quarter of the year.

The Trivial Many   The 80 percent in the 80:20 rule as devised by Vilfredo Pareto.

TheStreet.com   Popular web site that provides up-to-date stock market information and provocative investment articles by its editorial staff.

The Vital Few   The 20 percent in the 80:20 rule as devised by Vilfredo Pareto.

The Washington Service *(washserv.com)*   Web site that provides current information on insider filings, including a historical database of insider trades by company dating back to 1986.

Theory of Reflexivity   A two-way feedback mechanism in which reality shapes a participant's thinking, and the participant's thinking helps shape reality in an unending process. Developed by George Soros.

Glossary

200-day moving average   A technical indicator compiled as a statistical series of a security's closing price throughout 200 consecutive trading days. If a stock or index is above its 200-day moving average and the average is moving higher, a bullish trend exists. If the stock or index is below its 200-day moving average and the average is moving lower, a bearish trend exists. When prices are 20 percent or more below the 200-day moving average, an oversold condition exists, and a short-term rally could be expected.

Yahoo.com   A web site search engine that has a finance link that is very useful for investors as it provides company fundamentals and insider trading information.

Vilfredo Pareto   Nineteenth century Italian economist who observed that 80 percent of the national wealth in Italy was held by 20 percent of the people. In modern times, known as the 80:20 Rule. In business, most business managers believe that 80 percent of the sales and profits are generated by 20 percent of the people in the company, while at the same time 80 percent of a company's problems are caused by 20 percent of the employees.

Index

Index

Index

Index

Index

Index

Visit My Web Site

Please visit my web site: www.magict.info. To receive a weekly Magic T, you may subscribe to my subscription service for the individual investor. In addition to the weekly report, upon request, I will provide you with my insider insights to stocks, sectors, and industries of your interest. If you have general questions concerning my concept, please select the Contact Me option. I am determined to help you get maximum benefit from my book and/or my service.